22nd January 2004

To our very special Rebecca,
For your 22nd Birthday
in Chicago

Thank you for bringing us so much joy

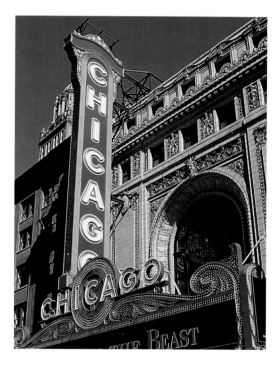

All our love

Mum & Dad

XXX

Phil 4 v 4

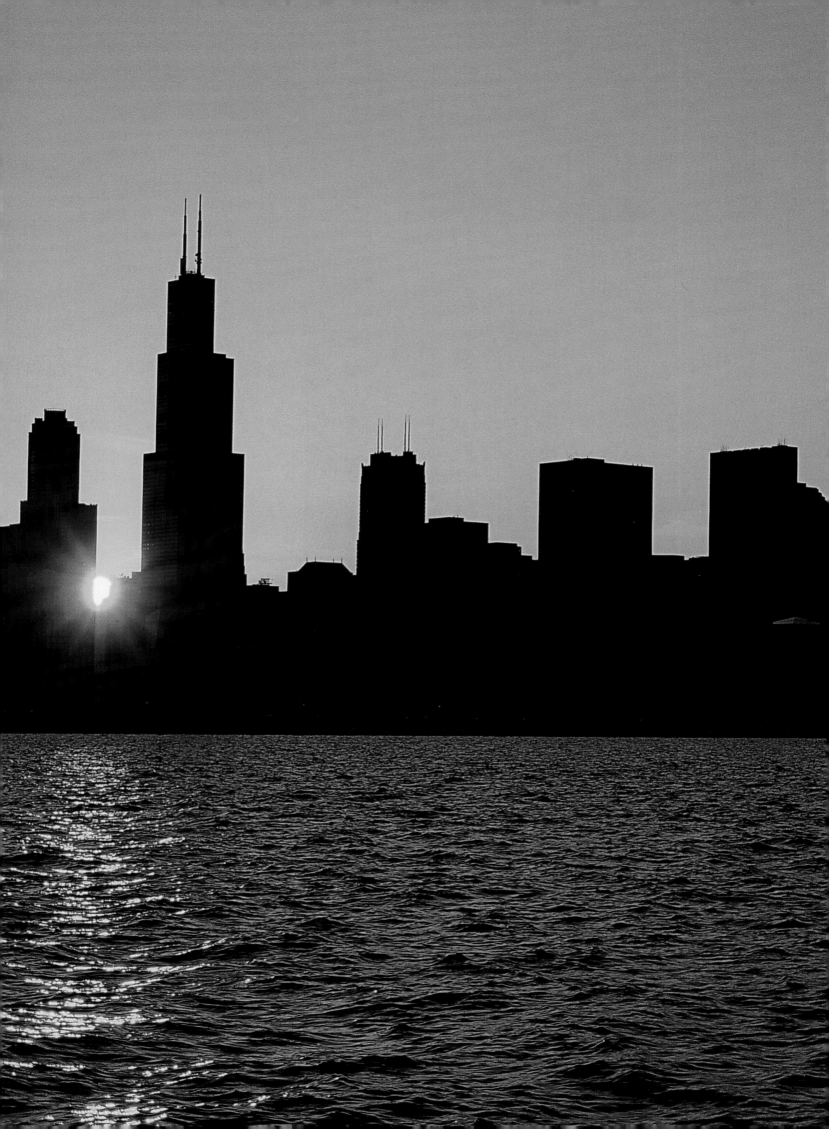

CHICAGO

A PHOTOGRAPHIC
CELEBRATION

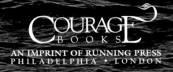

COURAGE
BOOKS

AN IMPRINT OF RUNNING PRESS
PHILADELPHIA • LONDON

Photography Credits

International Stock:

© Michael Girard: front cover , front flap and
   pp. 1, 2–3, 9, 13 (top, bottom left and right), 18,
   20–21, 22, 23, 24–25, 32–33, 34 (bottom), 35 (top
   and bottom), 38, 39 (top), 40, 42–43, 44 (top, bottom
   left and right), 45 (top and bottom), 49, 50–51, 52,
   53, 60 (top right and bottom), 61 (top, bottom left
   and right), 64 (bottom), 67 (top and bottom), 68–69,
   70, 71, 75, 78 (top left), 79 (top and bottom right),
   80, 81, 82 (top and bottom), 83 (top and bottom),
   86 (top), 89 (bottom), 96 (top right and bottom),
   97, 100, 101, 102 (top), 103 (top and bottom), 104,
   105 (top), 108 (top and bottom), 109, 111, 112–113,
   114 (top left, right, and bottom), 115, 116–117, 118
   (top and bottom), 119, 120, 121 (top left, right, and
   bottom), 122 (top left, right, and bottom), 123 (left
   and right), 124, 125 (top and bottom)

Grant Kessler Photography:

© Grant Kessler: back flap and pp. 8, 10–11, 16, 26,

28–29, 30, 31 (top and bottom), 34 (top), 64 (top),
78 (top right and bottom), 79 (bottom left), 92 (top),
93 (top and bottom), 96 (top left), 105 (bottom), 110

H. Armstrong Roberts:

© Werner Bertsch: pp. 89 (top), 90–91, 94–95

© J. Blank: pp. 46–47, 72–73

© Mark Gibson: p. 19 (top)

© Russell Kord: pp. 17, 36–37, 39 (bottom), 54–55,
   57, 60 (top left), 62–63, 65, 66, 74, 76–77, 84–85,
   86 (bottom), 87, 126–127, 128

© Ralph Krubner: p. 56

© Joseph Nettis: pp. 14–15, 41, 48, 88, 98–99

© P. Pearson: pp. 106–107

© Bill Ross: back cover and pp. 12, 27

© L. Smith: 92 (bottom), 102 (bottom)

© Adina Tovy: pp. 58–59

© W.R. Wright: p. 19 (bottom)

9 8 7 6 5 4 3 2
Digit on the right indicates the number of this printing

Library of Congress Cataloging-in-Publication Number 98-70511

ISBN 0-7624-0998-3

Cover design by Alicia Freile
Interior design by Corinda Cook
Photo research by Susan Oyama
Text by Marilyn Soltis
Typography: Caslon, Felix Titling, and Optima

Published by Courage Books, an imprint of
Running Press Book Publishers
125 South Twenty-second Street
Philadelphia, Pennsylvania 19103-4399

Visit us on the web!
www.runningpress.com

This book may be ordered by mail from the publisher.
But try your bookstore first!

(half-title page) The restored Chicago Theater movie house with it Beaux-Arts facade was reopened in 1986 for live-stage
productions with a performance by Frank Sinatra singing "My Kind of Town." Originally built for showmen Balaban & Katz,
the Chicago Theater still retains much of its movie palace glamour.

(title page) The dramatic Chicago skyline at dusk showcases some of the world's most innovative architecture including
the famous Sears Tower, which competes for billing as the tallest building in the world.

IT'S THE NATION'S third largest city, but Chicago is world-class in every way. Some of the world's tallest skyscrapers rise up next to miles of lakefront parks and sandy beaches. Renowned museums, an internationally acclaimed symphony orchestra, elegant shops, and sophisticated restaurants and theater are among its many attractions. Sports are big here, from the victorious Chicago Bulls to the less successful but ever popular Chicago Cubs.

This most American of cities has a colorful history full of titans of industry, gangsters, crooked politicians, musicians, and an assortment of immigrants from every corner of the world. It was first discovered by Father Marquette and Louis Joliet when they were sent by the King of France to find a water route between the Mississippi River and Lake Michigan in 1673. Chicago was a swamp named "Chicagou" by the Indians, which meant "the stink of garlic and wild onions."

Fur traders populated the area when the town was incorporated about 1833 with a population of only a few hundred. By the 1850s, it had become an important railroad center. During the Civil War, many of its men fought under Abraham Lincoln in the Union Army. It continued to prosper after the war with several important companies emerging, such as Sears Roebuck & Co. and Montgomery Ward's.

By 1890, the city had grown to more than a million people, a popular destination for the steady stream of immigrants into the country. They came to find work in Chicago's teaming factories and stench-filled stockyards, made notorious by Upton Sinclair's 1906 novel "The Jungle." There were Germans, Poles, Croats, Slavs, Jews, Italians, Blacks, Greeks, Asians, and Latins, among others. Most of them lived together and formed the basis of many of the ethnic neighborhoods that retain their original essence today—neighborhoods such as Ukrainian Village, Little Italy, Chinatown, and Greektown.

Tremendous fortunes were being made by entrepreneurs like Pullman, Armour, Swift, and McCormick. In 1871, the Great Chicago Fire burned three and a half square miles of the city to the ground. More than seventeen thousand buildings were destroyed. But the spirit of the city was strong. It rose from the ashes quickly and became even greater than before. It was a town of paradoxes with a vibrant underbelly of gamblers, prostitutes, wild artists, sculptors, and yellow journalists. It was also home to Hull House founders Jane Addams and Elizabeth Gates Starr and an ever-active Women's Christian Temperance Union led by Frances E. Willard.

The Great Fire also created a new vista for the architects that flocked to the windy city, seeing the opportunity to create a new vision. That new vision was what is now known as the Chicago School of Architecture. The tradition was set by architectural giants like Louis Henry Sullivan, John Wellborn Root, and William Holabird. In 1885, William LeBaron Jenney used steel frame construction for the Home Insurance Building, which has since been torn down, for what is now considered the forerunner to the modern skyscraper. Frank Lloyd Wright transformed the idea of single-family homes; many of his structures can still be toured in Oak Park. Later, Ludwig Mies van der Rohe greatly influenced modern architecture in Chicago and around the world. Today, many of the world's tallest skyscrapers dominate the Chicago skyline—the Sears Tower, Standard Oil Building, and John Hancock Center among them.

Throughout the city, stunning churches and synagogues can be found even in the most humble neighborhoods. St. Mary of the Angels Catholic Church opened in Bucktown around 1920 and is modeled after St. Peter's Basilica in Rome. The Fourth Presbyterian Church on Michigan Avenue is a magnificent Gothic Revival building that went up in 1914. In Old Town, St. Michael's Church bells still ring in the now upscale neighborhood. Rockefeller Chapel at the University of Chicago is a stunning tribute to Gothic architecture.

At the beginning of the century, great department stores like Marshall Field's and Carson Pirie Scott, which still dominate State Street, dictated fashions. Audiences filled the Auditorium Theater, Opera House, and Chicago Theater as they still do today. The 1920s and early 30s were the heyday of bootleg criminals like Alphonse "Scarface" Capone, Bugs Moran, Hymie Weiss, and Big Jim Colosino, whose reputations still mark Chicago as a land of gangsters to the outside world.

At the same time in history, jazz greats like Benny Goodman, Louis Armstrong, and the Dorsey Brothers were making Chicago a well known jazz center. Some of the country's best blues clubs still dot the nightlife scene here. A number of great writers came out of Chicago, notably Nelson Algren, Richard Wright, and James Farrell.

Many of Chicago's great institutions are rooted in the past. The Art Institute with its stunning collection of Impressionist paintings, the Museums of Science and Industry and Natural History, the Shedd Aquarium, and the Adler Planetarium are still Chicago's premier tourist attractions. Due to the vision of great men like Montgomery Ward, the lakefront parks were preserved for everyone, not just the privileged classes. Daniel Burnham designed Grant Park in 1920 to resemble the gardens at Versailles and kept the lakefront unobstructed. Kate Buckingham donated the Beaux-Arts style Buckingham Fountain in memory of her brother, Clarence.

It is hard to find a city more culturally diverse than Chicago. It has always been known as the city of neighborhoods, and the gentrification of the 1990s has not eradicated the character of these enclaves. Once again the city, which saw an exodus to the suburbs during the 1950s, 60s, and 70s, is seeing renewed growth and prosperity that radiates from the Loop in every direction.

Many historic neighborhoods retain their charm and architectural significance. From Lincoln Park to Rogers Park, from the South Loop to Hyde Park and from River West to Wicker Park, new generations of settlers are rejuvenating the early settlements.

Artists and real estate speculators have transformed the Bucktown/Wicker Park area which is teeming with historical atmosphere. A neighborhood hangout like the original Rainbo Club was also a regular place for writers Nelson Algren and Simone de Beauvoir to stop for a drink. Restored mansions built by upscale merchants at the turn of the century line several blocks. Not far away are redone worker's bungalows where there used to be so many goats grazing that the area was nicknamed "Bucktown." It was also the setting for many of Algren's characters. Funky coffeehouses next to trendy restaurants abound along with art galleries, music clubs, boutiques, bakeries, and shops. It is also a hotbed of filmmakers and musicians.

The South Loop, a long a deserted pocket, is experiencing another renaissance. An entire new community of lofts, townhouses, and single-family homes is popping up where old warehouses and factories once predominated. Little Italy, around the University of Illinois, has been transformed from an immigrant community to a chic neighborhood. North side neighborhoods all seem to be in a chronic state of rehabilitation with new construction, vintage renovation, and new businesses.

"The Magnificent Mile" is truly one of the world's great shopping meccas. Michigan Avenue offers luxury hotels, fine restaurants, and representation by an array of international stores. Not far from the Mag Mile is Navy Pier, the recently renovated mile-long promontory that juts out onto Lake Michigan.

The "Windy City" wasn't named after the brutal winds of the lake. (Bad weather is just part of the charm.) The name came from a reporter during the World's Columbian Exposition in 1893, because everyone bragged about the place so much.

We think you'll see why.

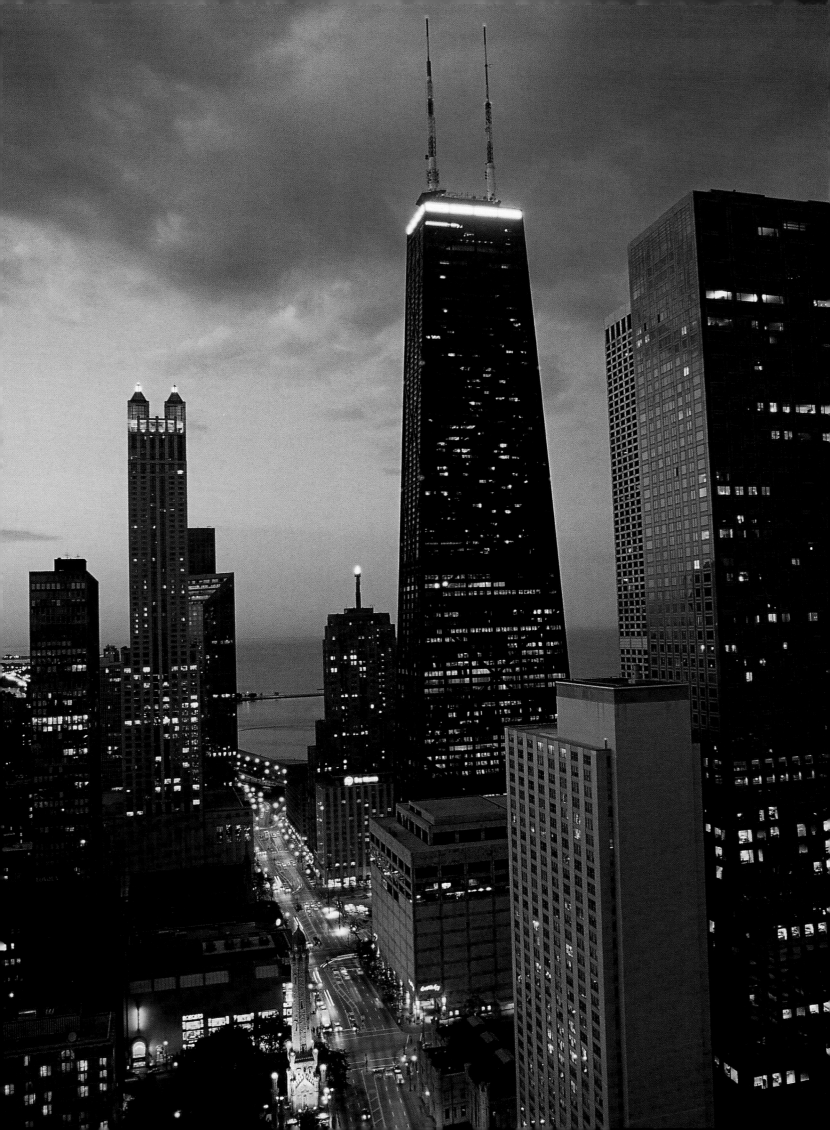

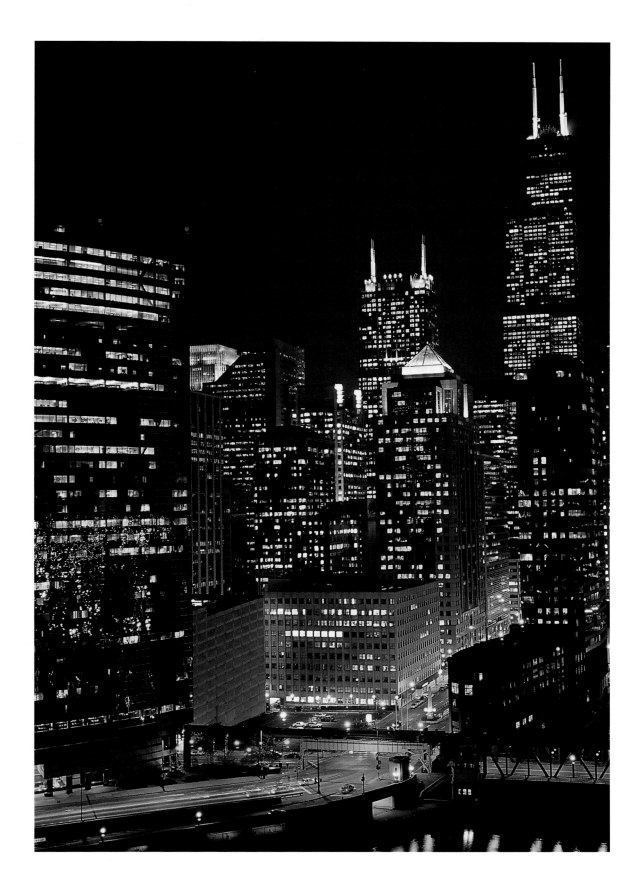

(left) "Magnificent Mile" with the Hancock tower, built in 1969, and Water Tower place.

(above) Chicago's riverfront with the Sears Tower standing tall.

(overleaf) "Big John" Hancock Center and vicinity.

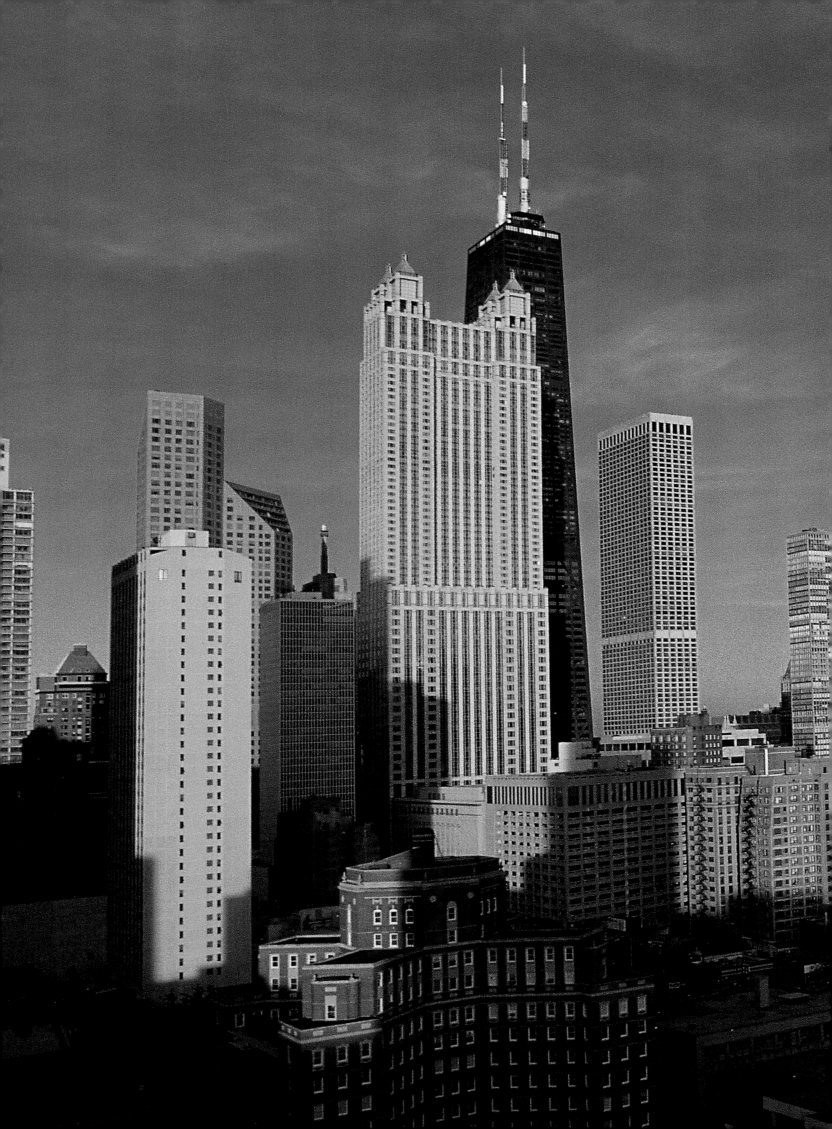

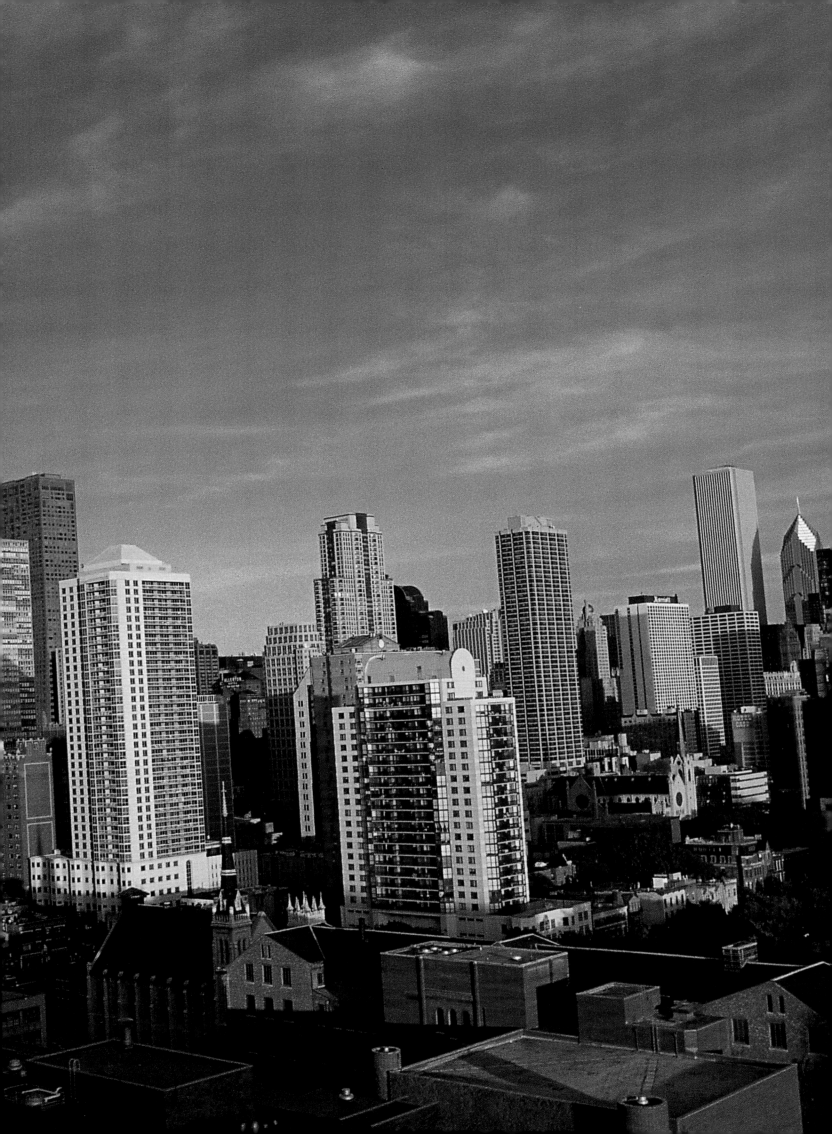

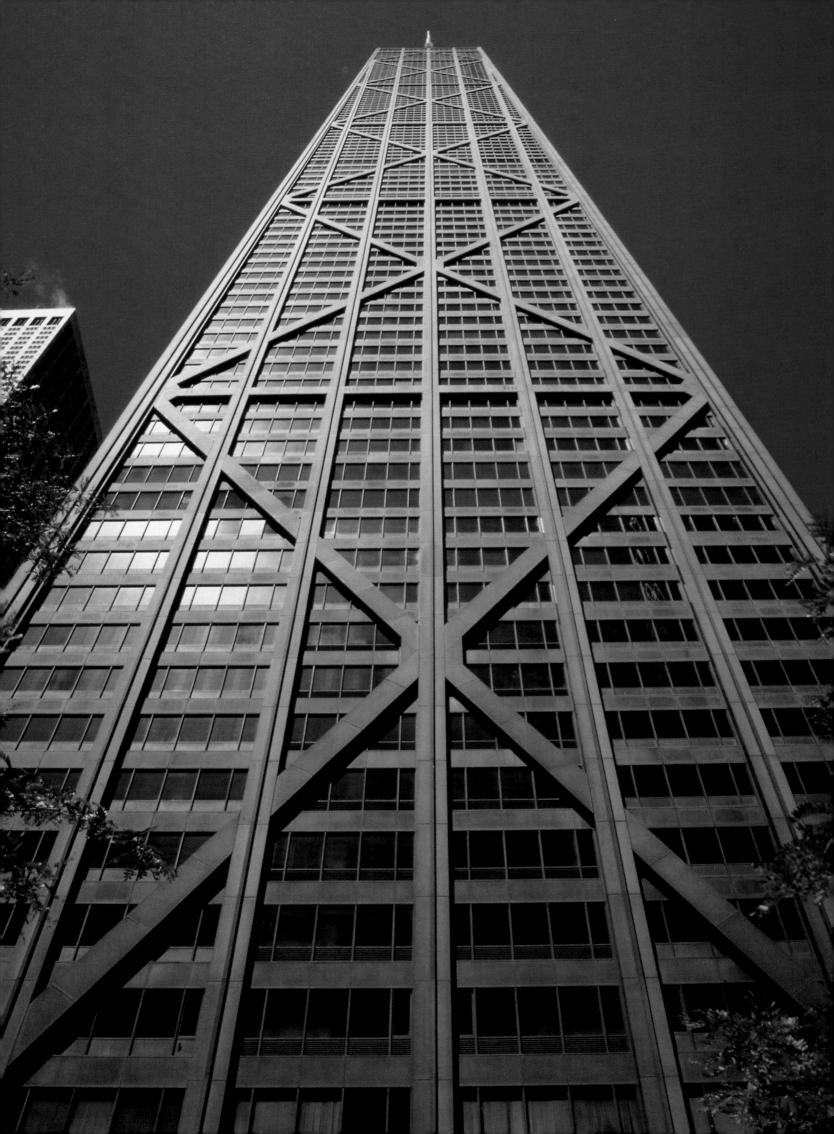

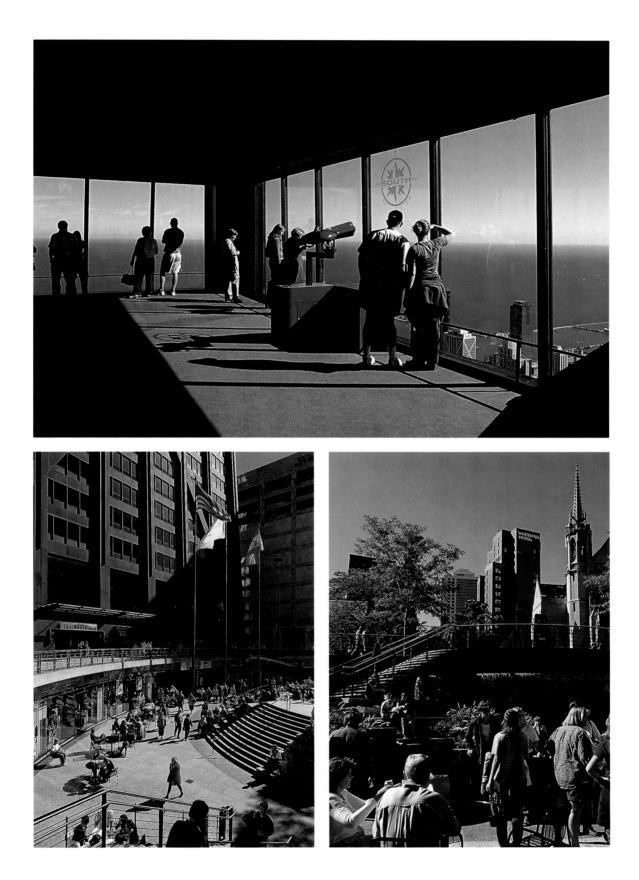

(far left) The John Hancock Center. **(top)** The 1,127-foot-high observatory atop the Hancock tower.

(bottom left and right) The shops and restaurant at the base of the Hancock tower are a popular tourist destination along "Magnificent Mile."

(overleaf) The Hancock Center observatory offers a breathtaking view of Chicago's famous lakefront.

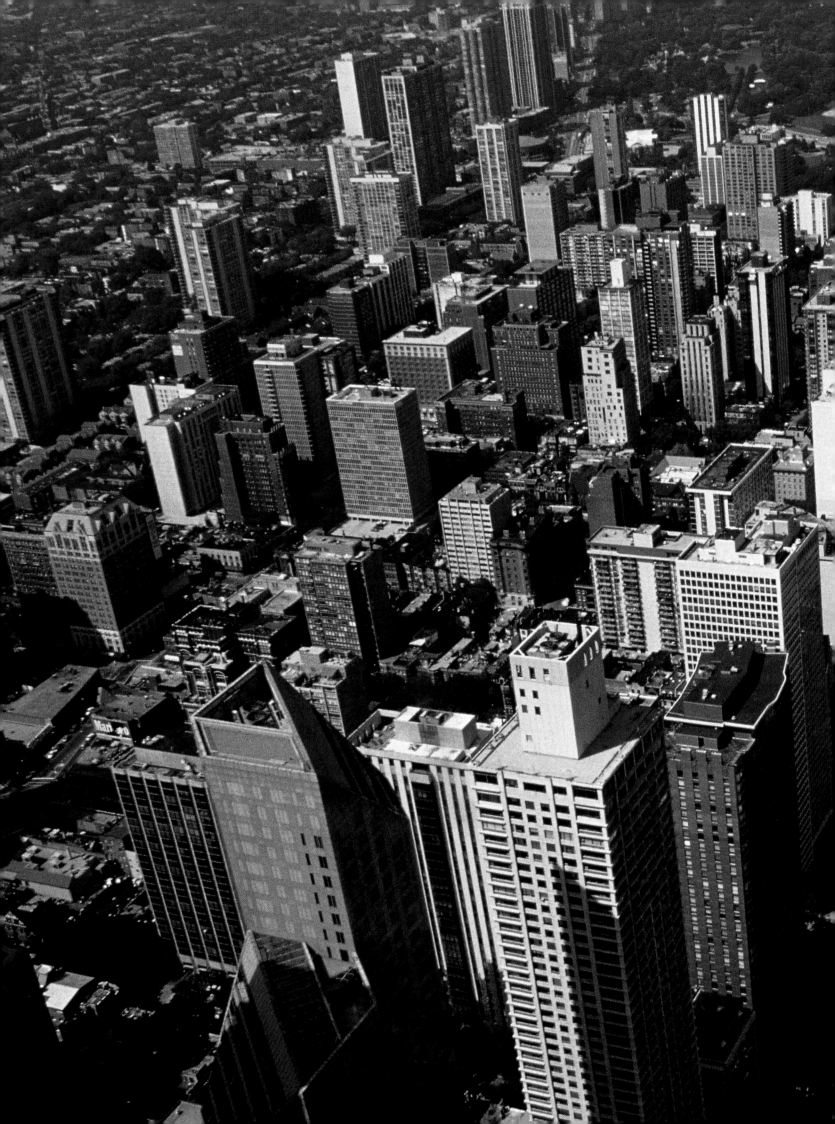

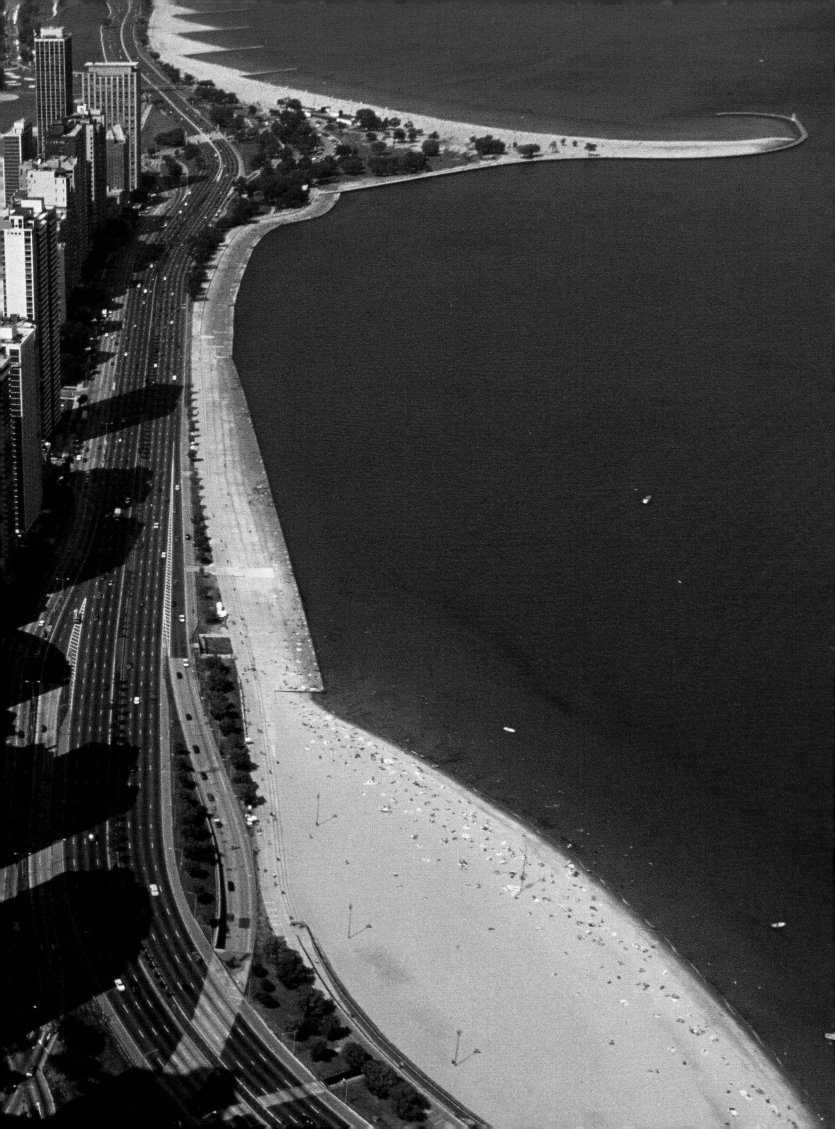

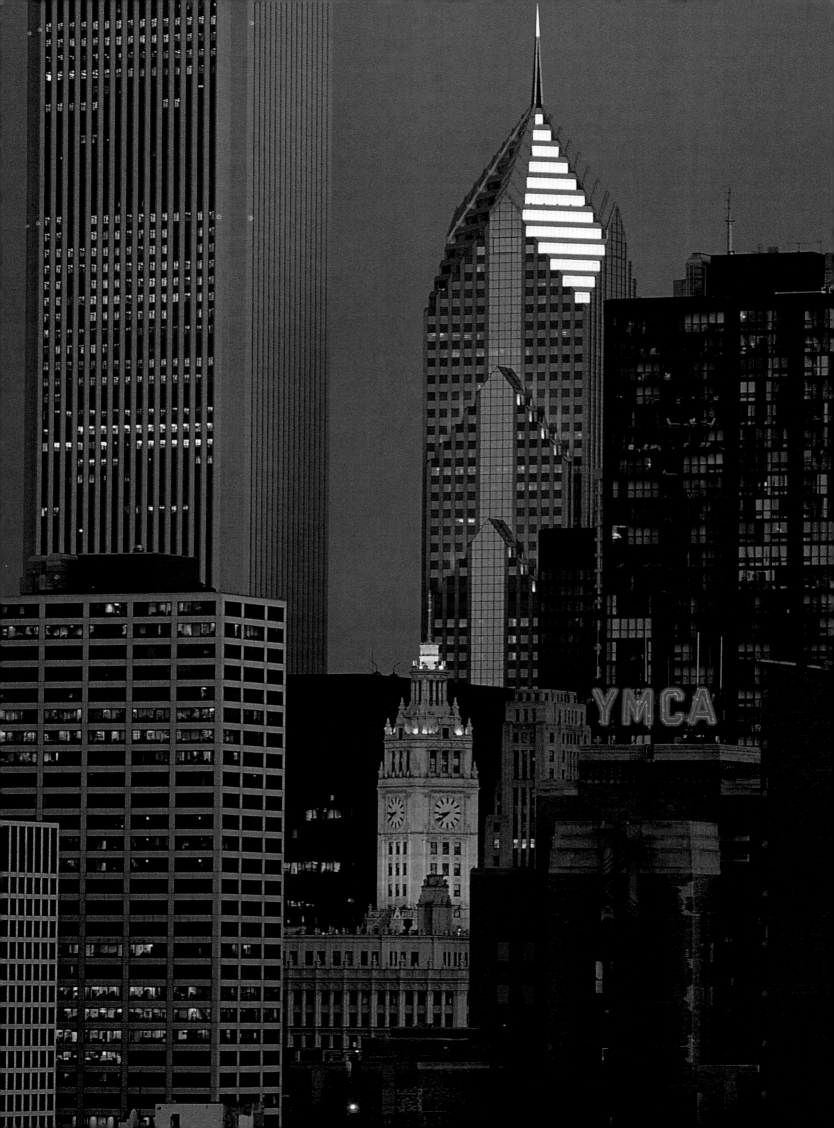

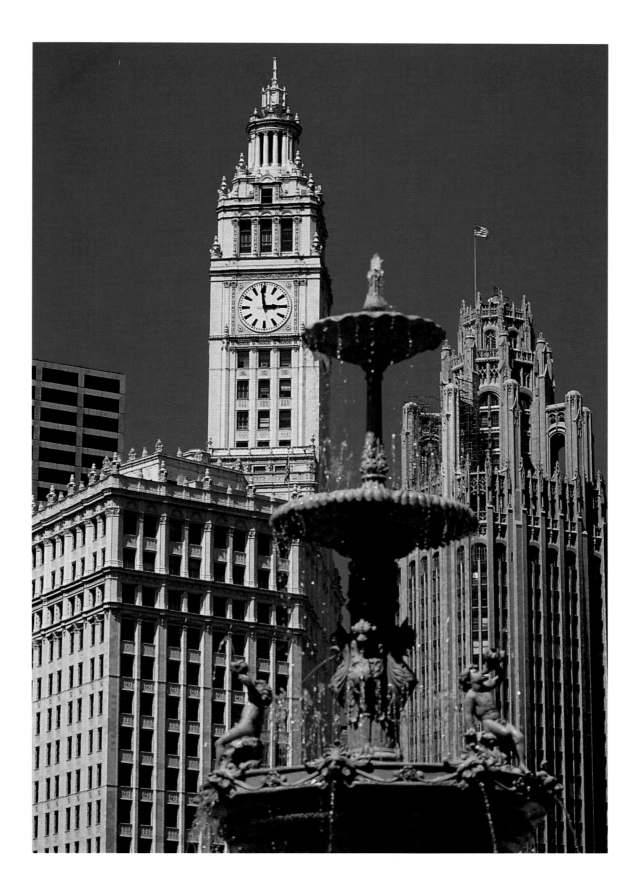

(left) Formerly called the Amoco Building, the 80-story Aon Center, on the far left, is Chicago's second tallest structure. The 42-story Prudential Building, with its gleaming pyramid top, was erected in 1955 and was for many years the city's tallest building.

(above) The Wrigley Building, built by the chewing-gum king, and *Chicago Tribune* tower.

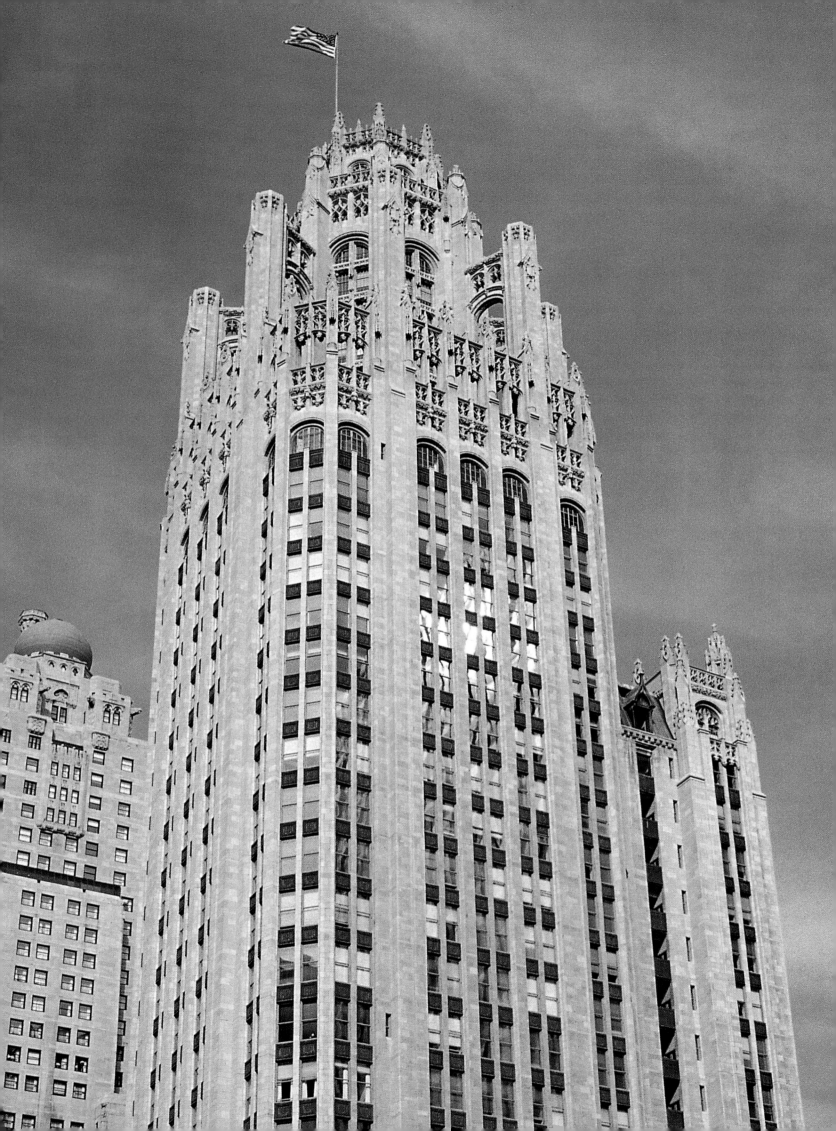

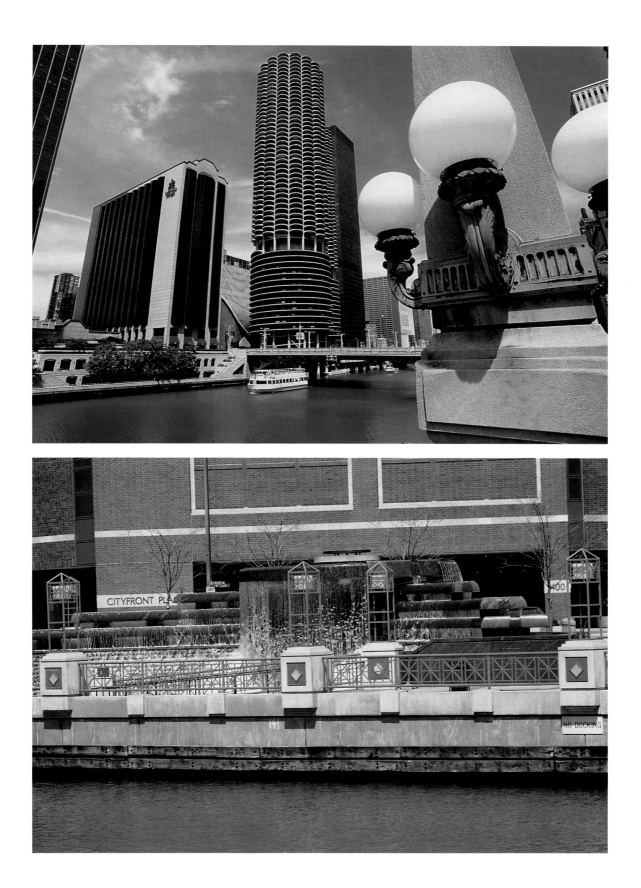

(left) The *Tribune* tower, a gothic revival skyscraper built in 1922.

(above) Chicago's river walk provides a pleasant thoroughfare for a leisurely stroll or a meal at a waterfront restaurant.

(overleaf) There are 43 bridges crossing the Chicago River. Twenty of them are located in the downtown area. The Chicago River is an essential link in a chain of waterways running from the Great Lakes to the Gulf of Mexico.

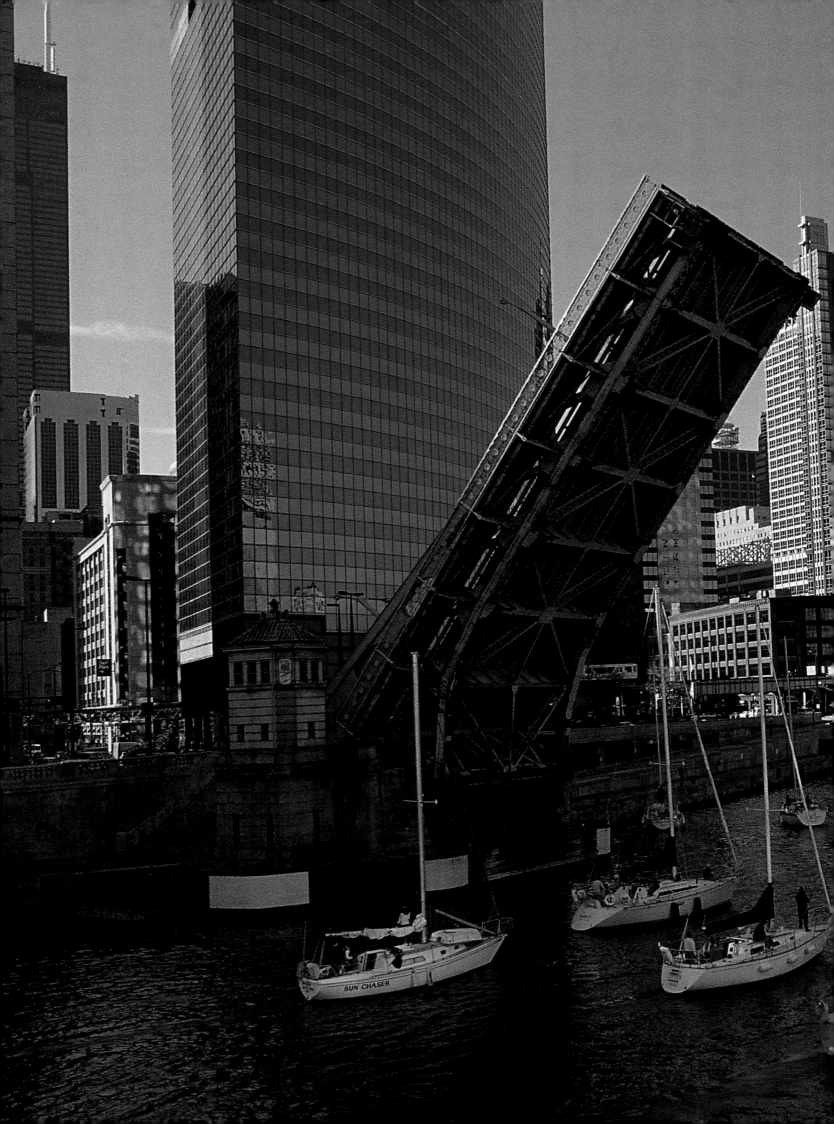

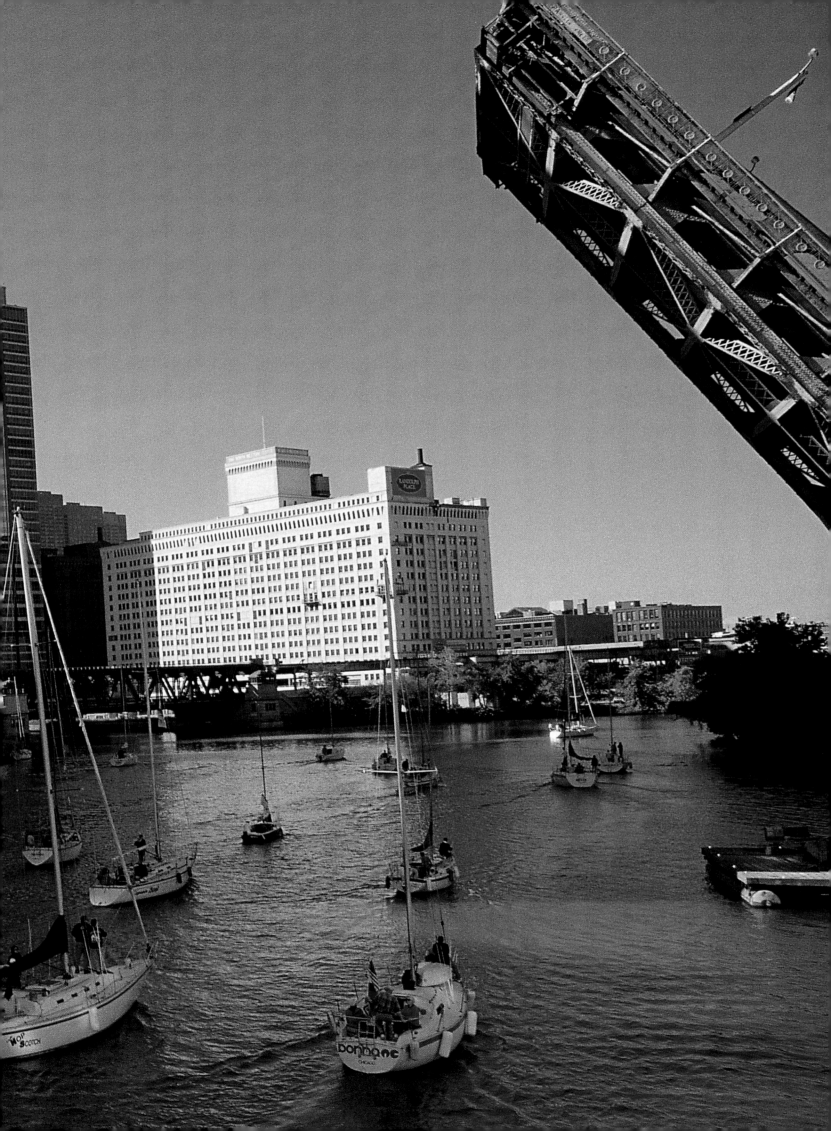

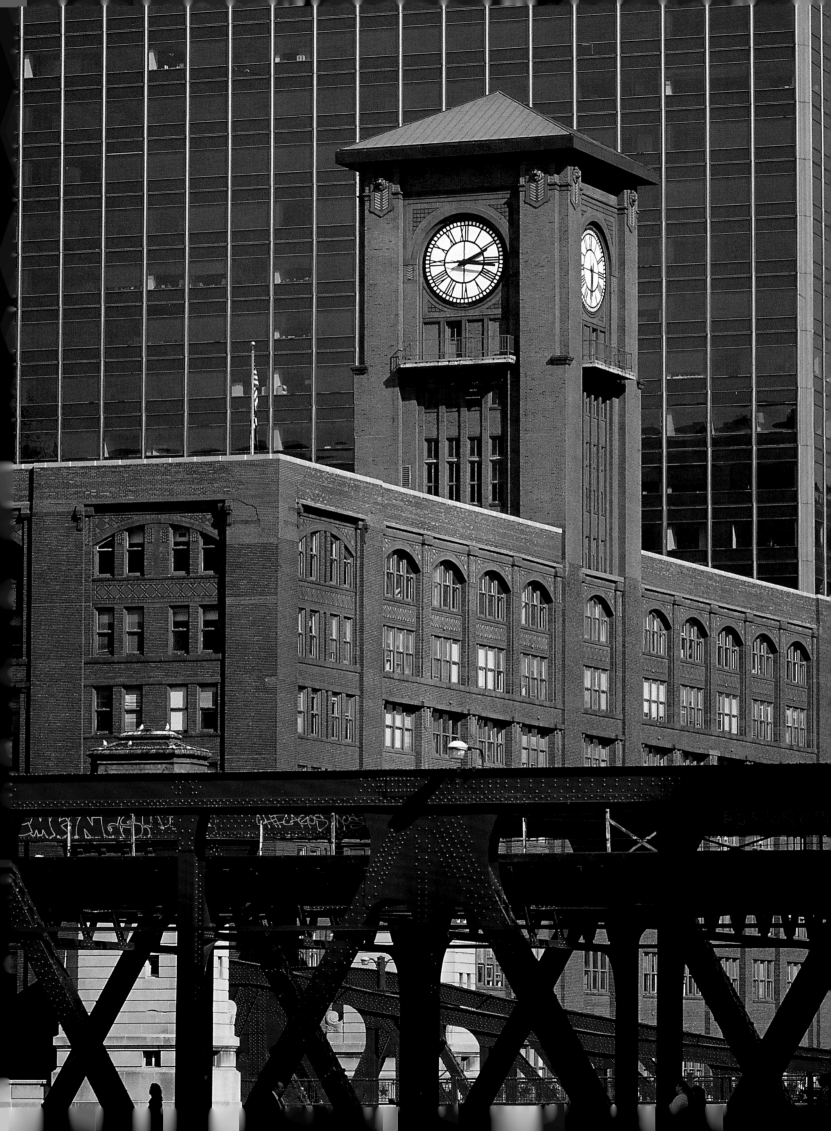

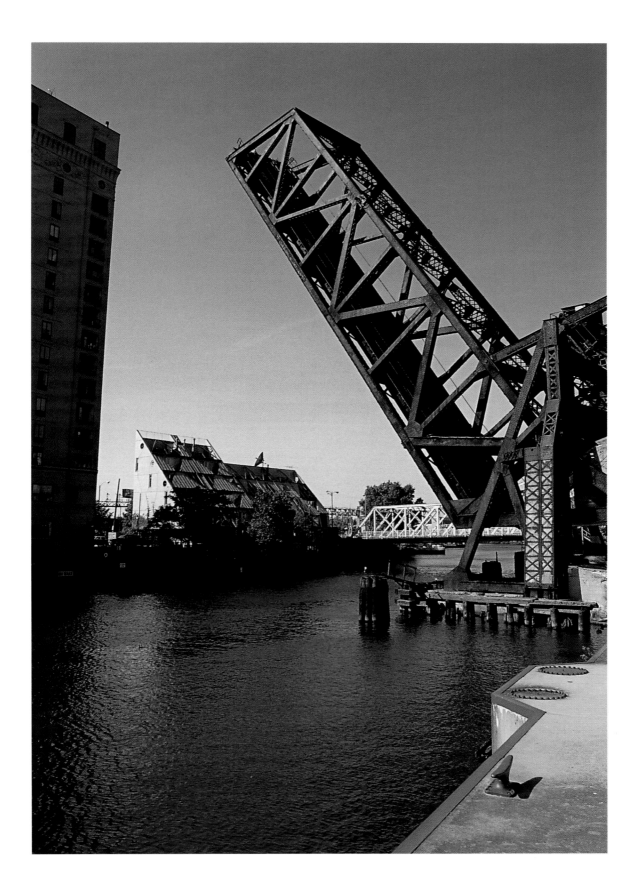

(**left**) The Traffic Court Building stands out in the River North neighborhood with its unique clock tower.

(**above**) The Kinzie Bridge—River North.

(**overleaf**) Chicago River—Wells Street Bridge.

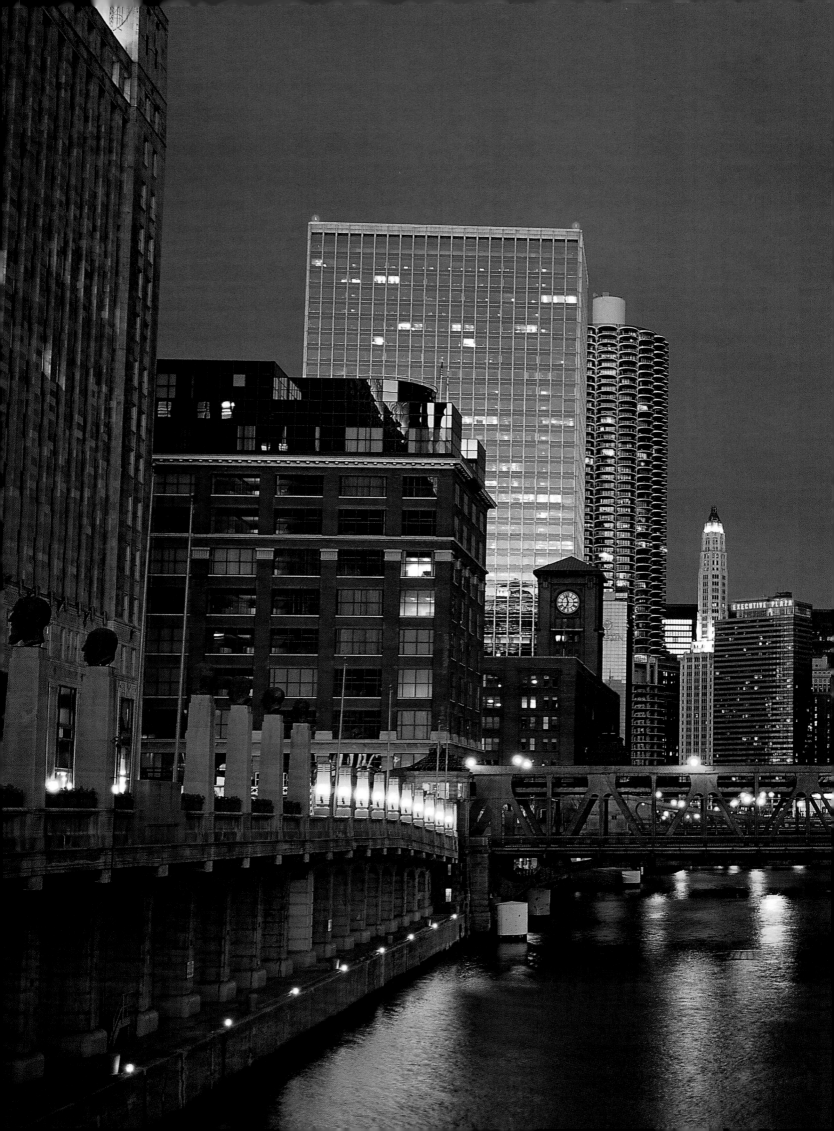

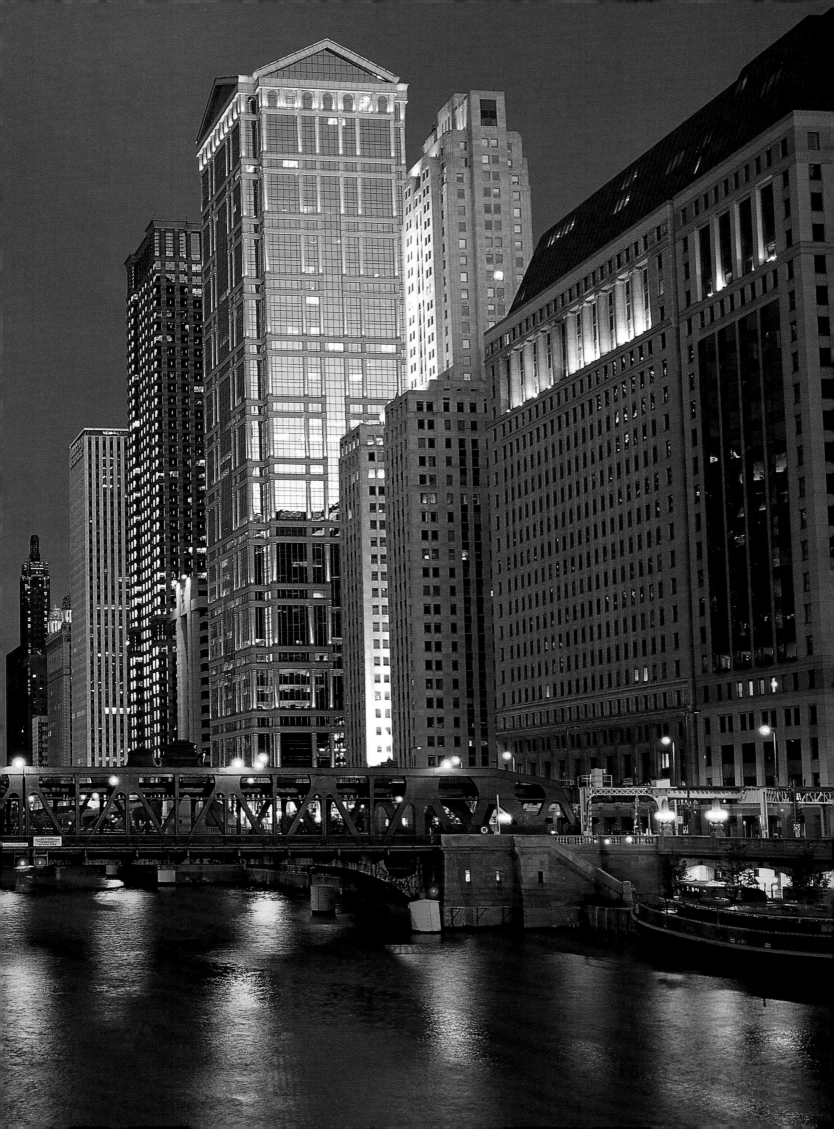

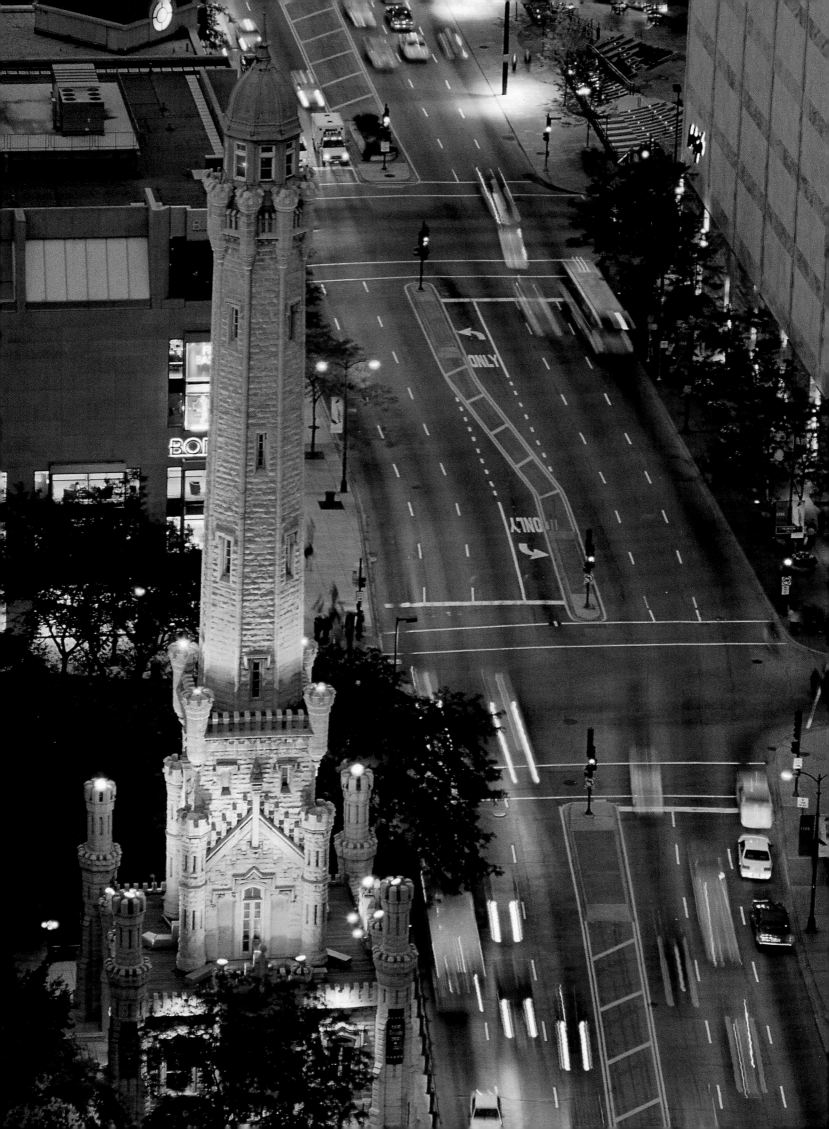

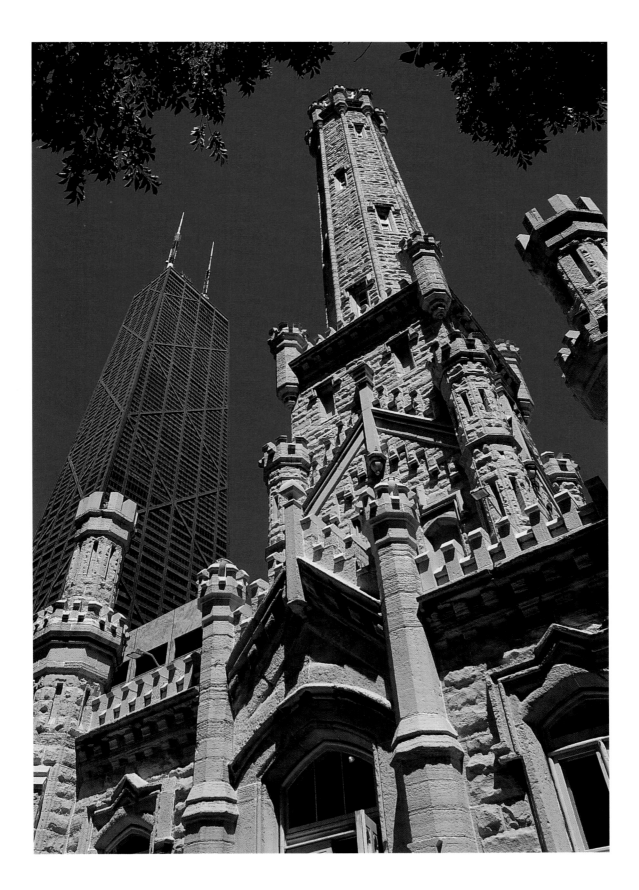

(left and above) Chicago's historic Water Tower was completed in 1869. Two years later, it was the only structure to survive the Great Fire that decimated the city.

(overleaf) The Streeterville skyline glows eerily at night, partially illuminated by Navy Pier and its 150-foot-tall Ferris wheel.

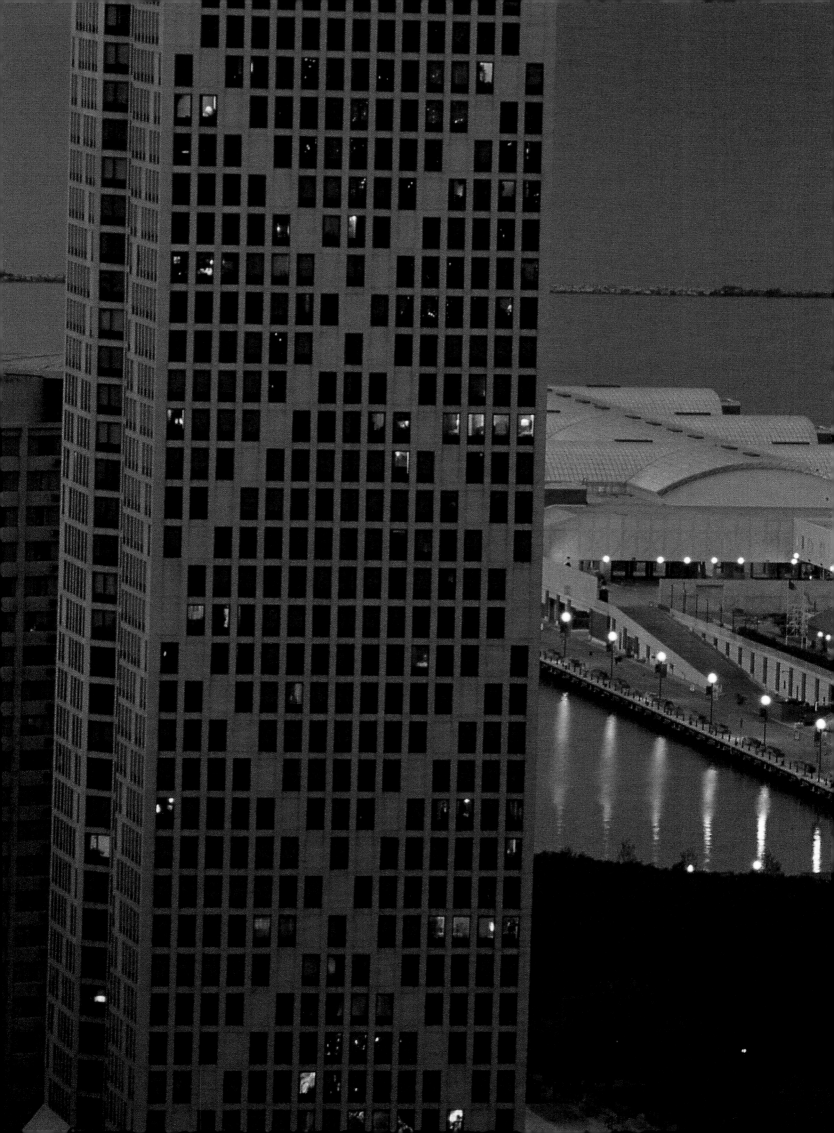

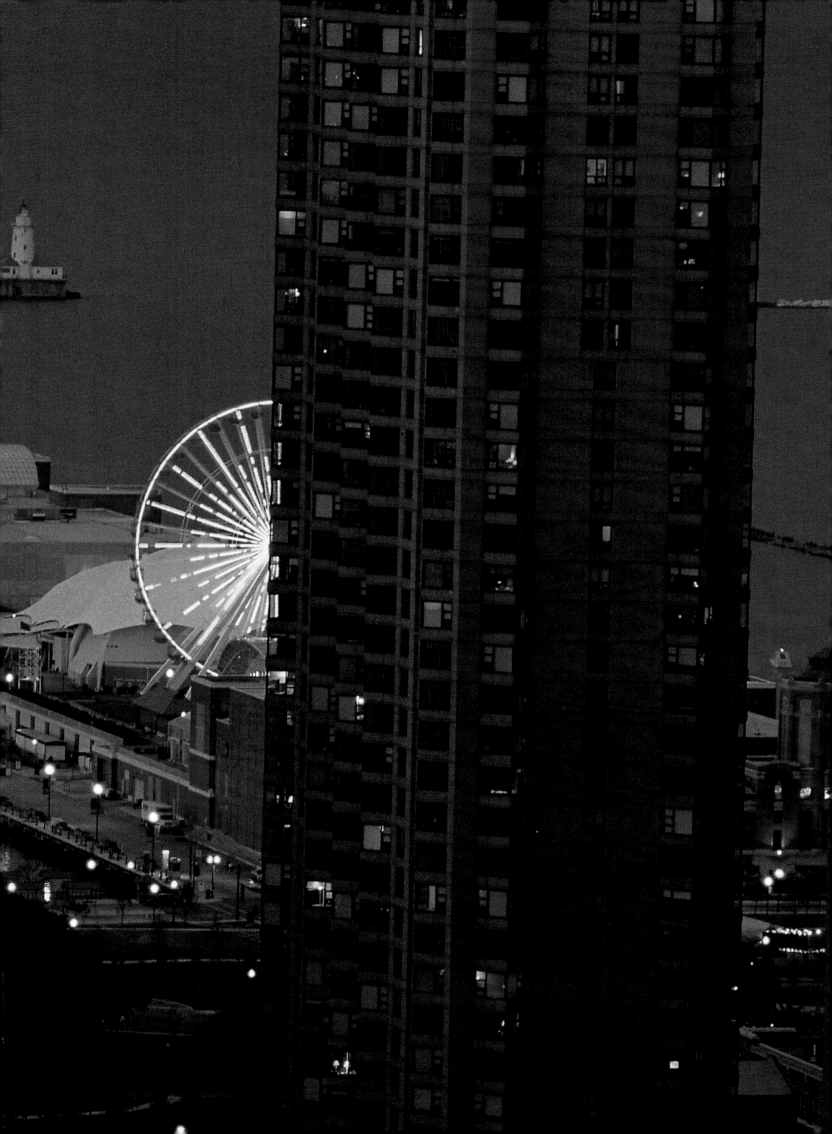

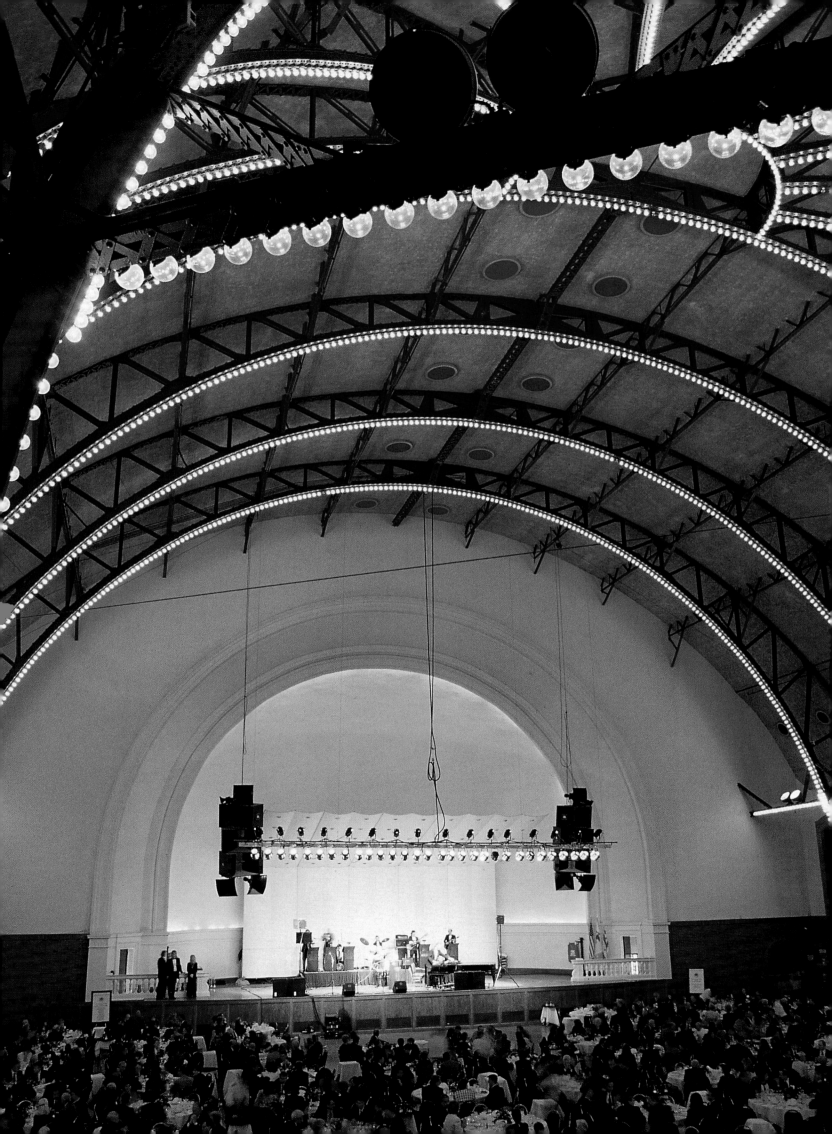

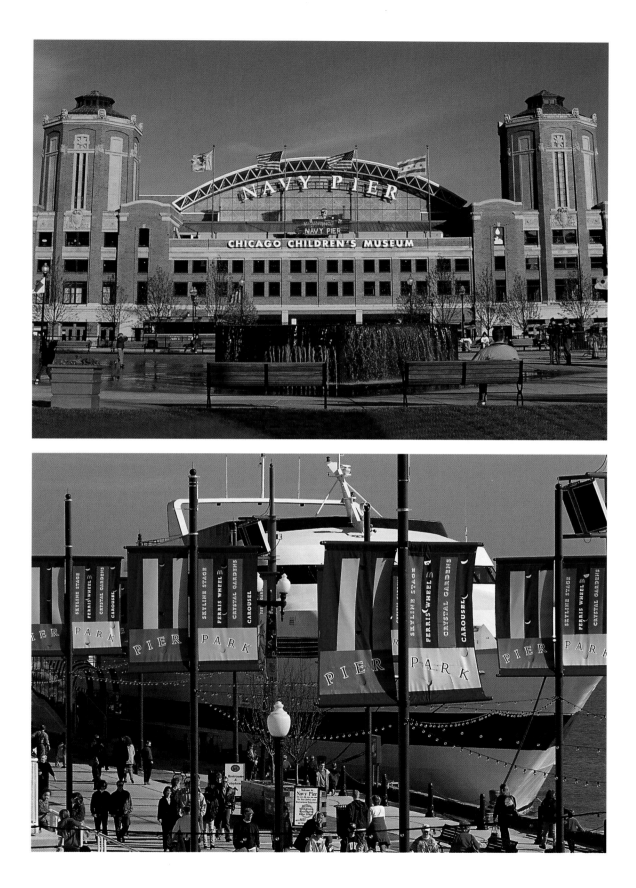

(left) Navy Pier Ballroom. (top) Navy Pier Children's Museum. (above) Navy Pier.

(overleaf) Navy Pier Ferris wheel.

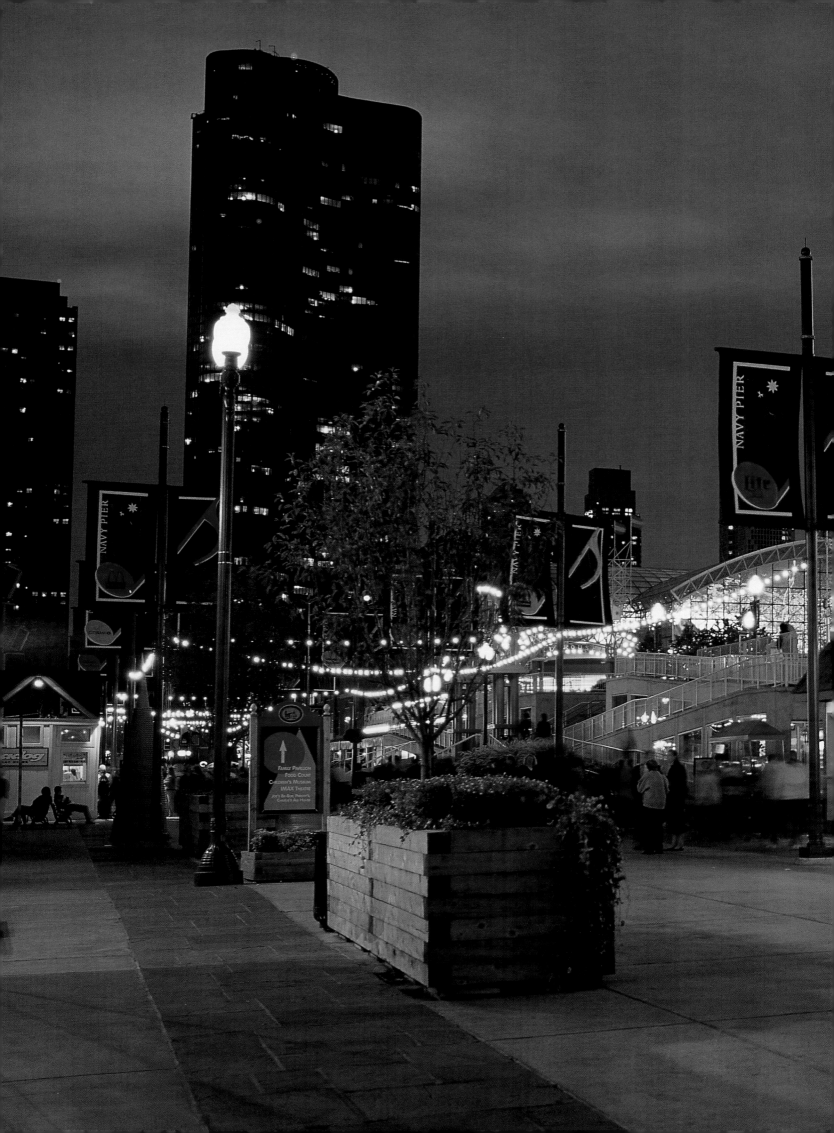

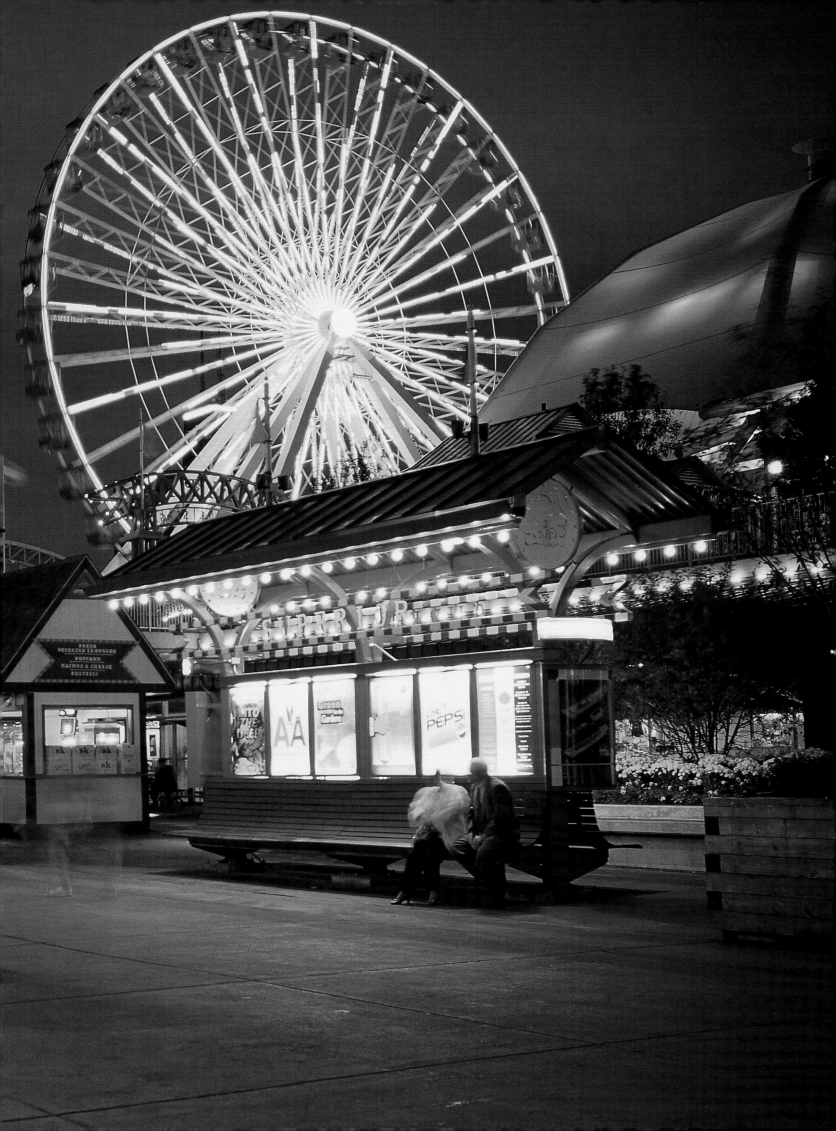

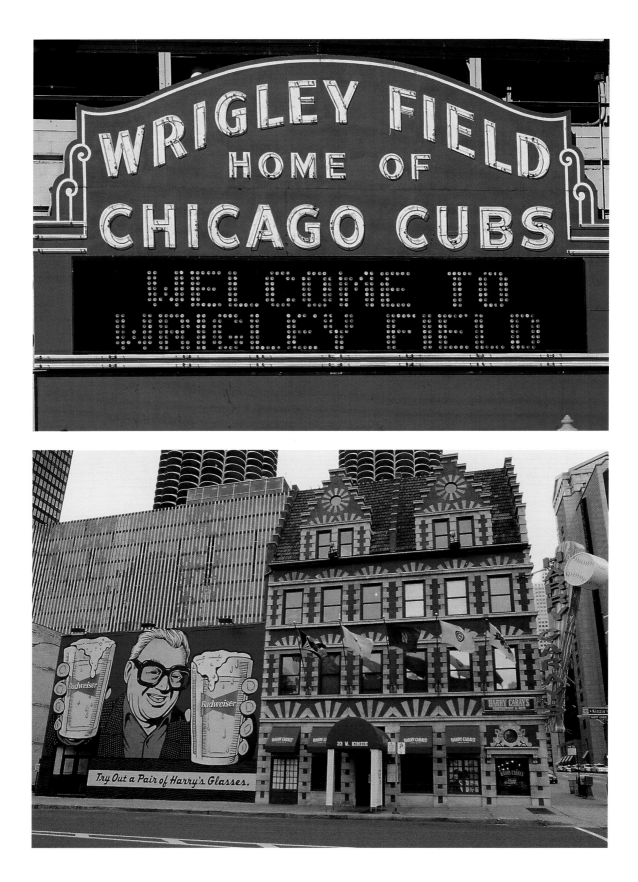

(top) Hope springs eternal at Wrigley Field, home to the Chicago Cubs. The team's record never affects attendance, with sold-out games all summer long.

(bottom) Harry Carey's restaurant: Sports memorabilia fills the former Cub's announcer's restaurant in the River North neighborhood.

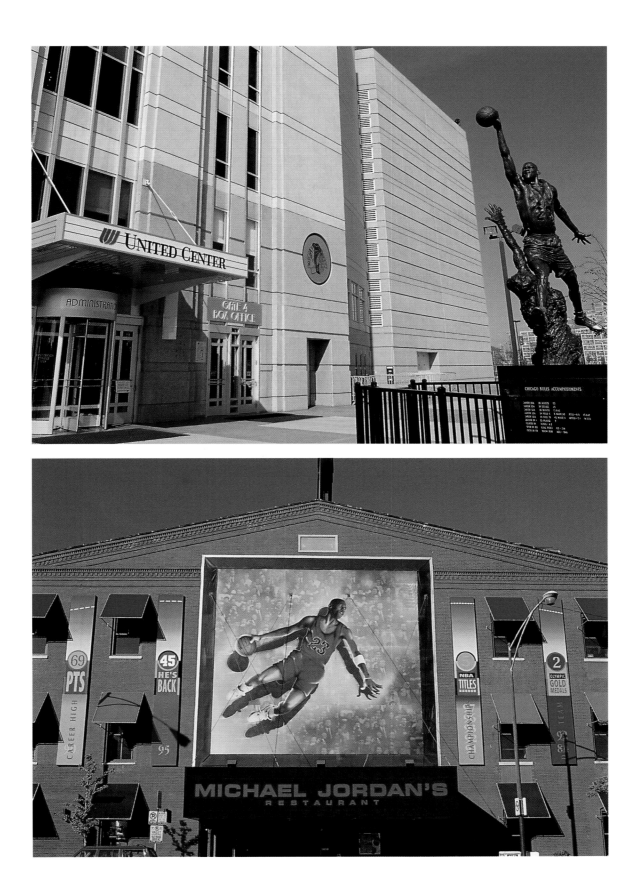

(top) Some say this is the house Michael Jordan built: the new United Center, home to the Chicago Bulls.

(bottom) Michael Jordan's restaurant: You might not spot him here, but the restaurant is filled with interesting memorabilia.

(overleaf) Intricate detailing and stone work adds to the graceful dignity of the former LaSalle Street entrance arch of the old Stock Exchange. It is now displayed in the East Garden of the Art Institute.

35

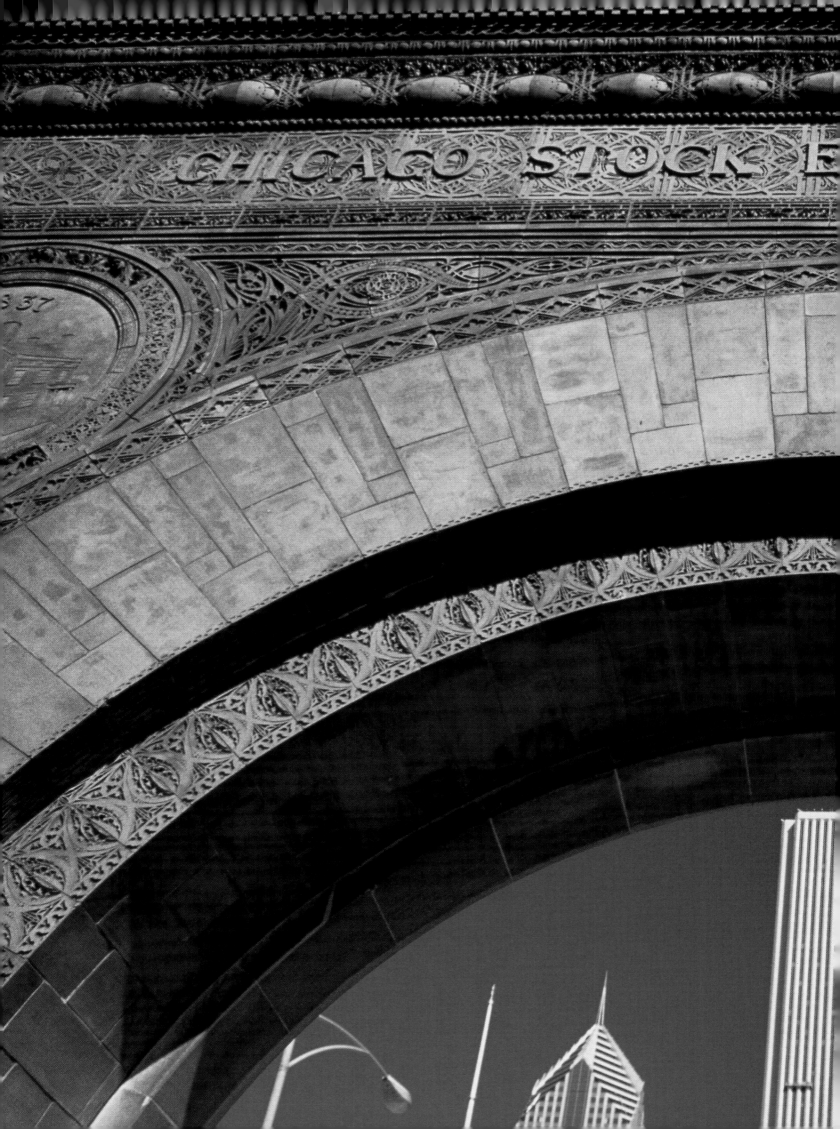

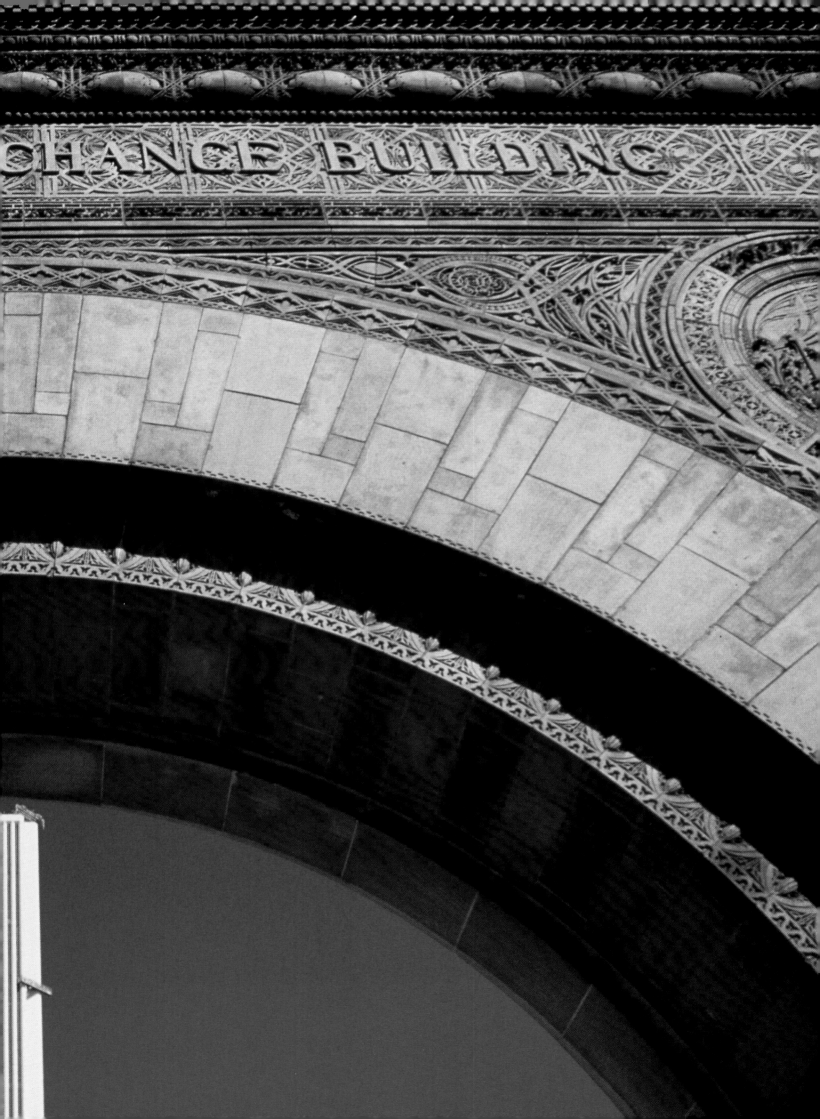

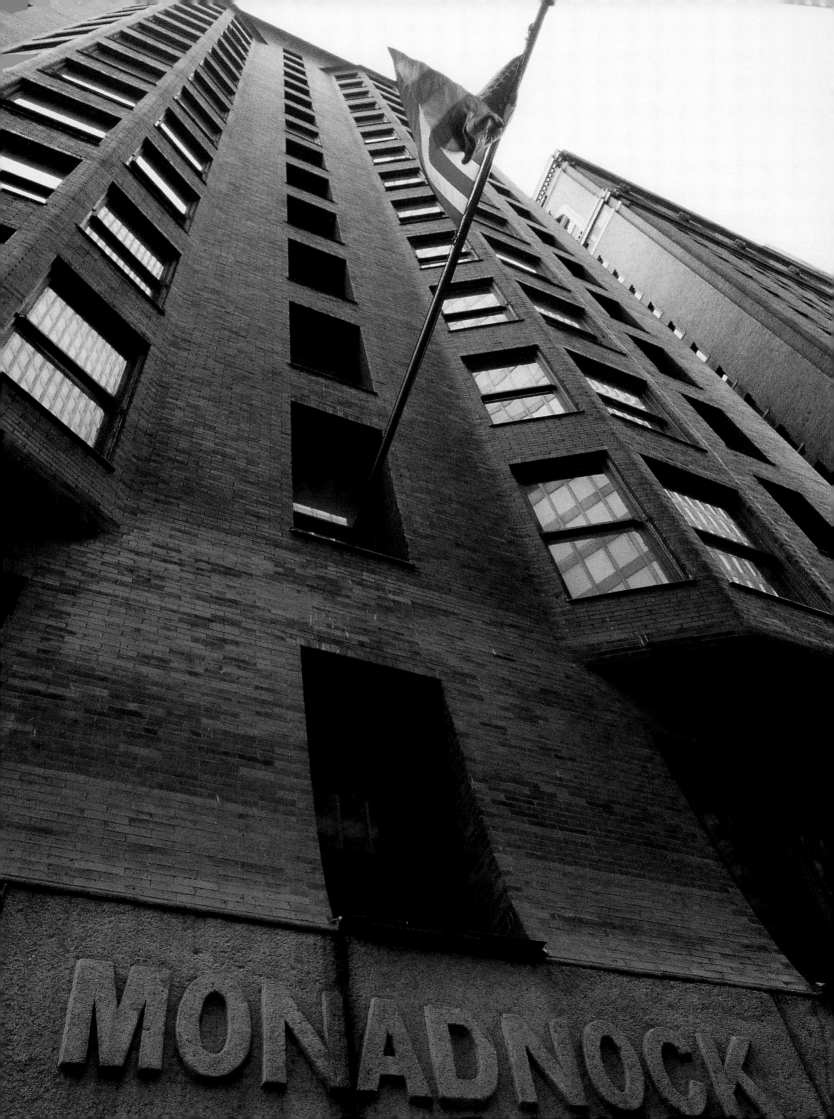

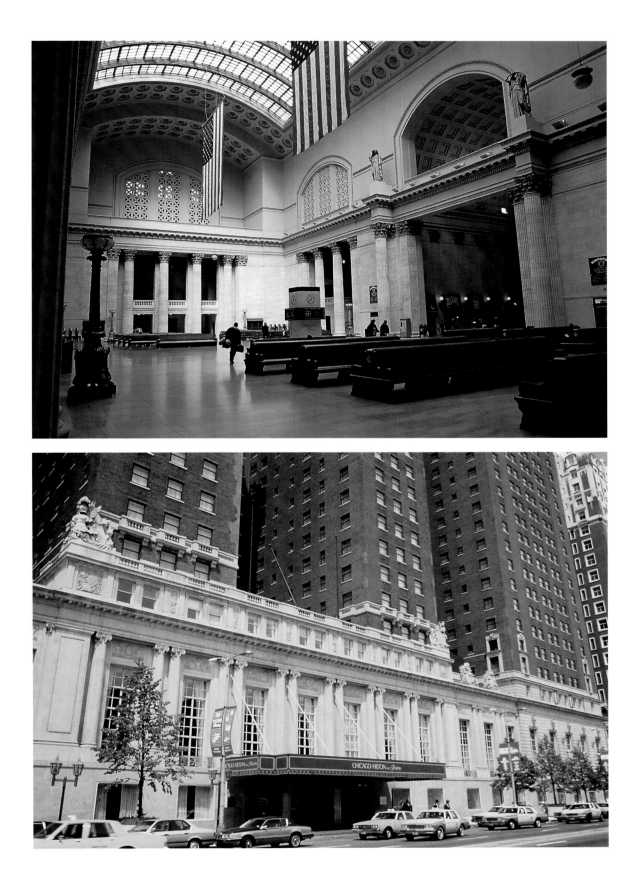

(left) Monadnock building.

(top) Union Station interior.

(bottom) Chicago Hilton and Tower.

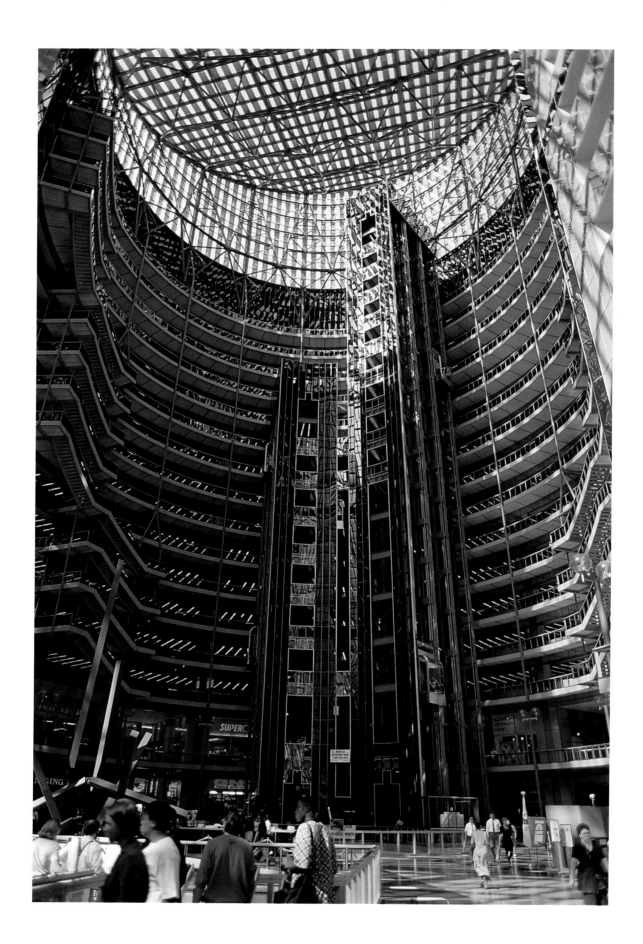

(above and right) The James R. Thompson Center and Jean Dubuffet's 20-foot-high fiberglass sculpture, "Monument with Standing Beast" in the plaza below.

(overleaf) The 25-story Merchandise Mart, which covers two city blocks and is the largest commercial building in the world.

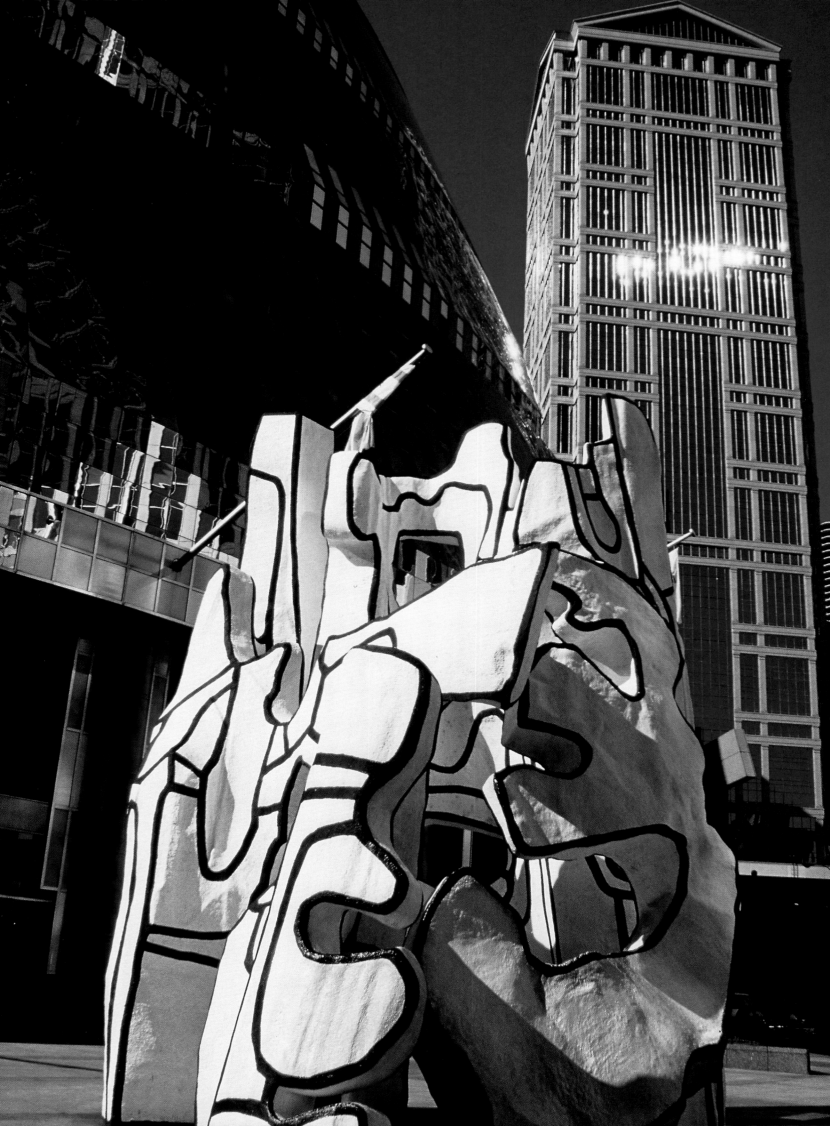

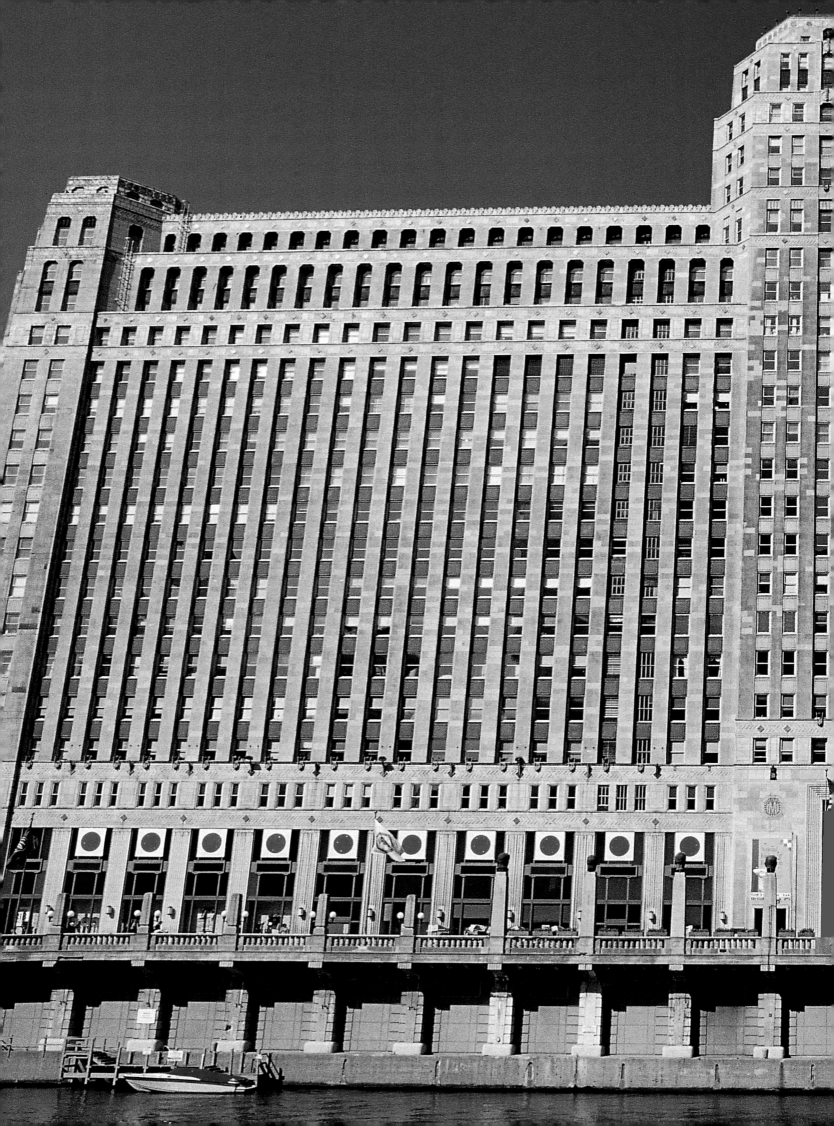

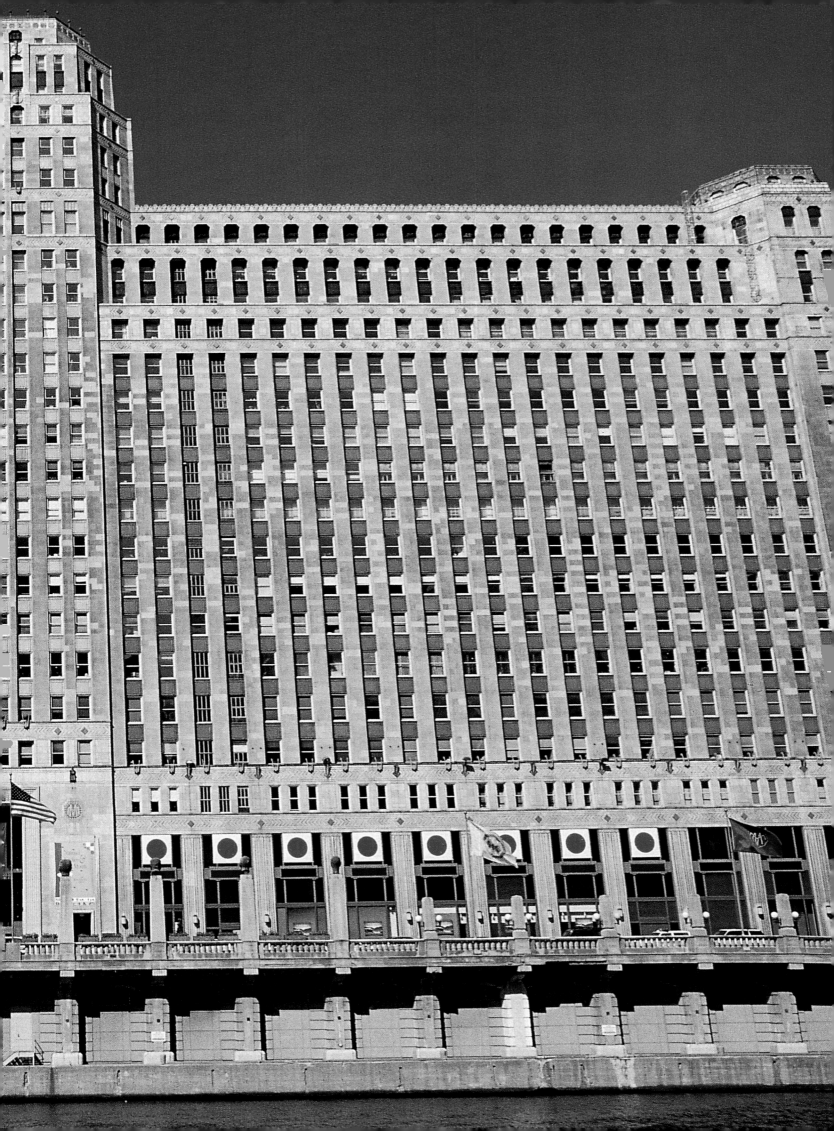

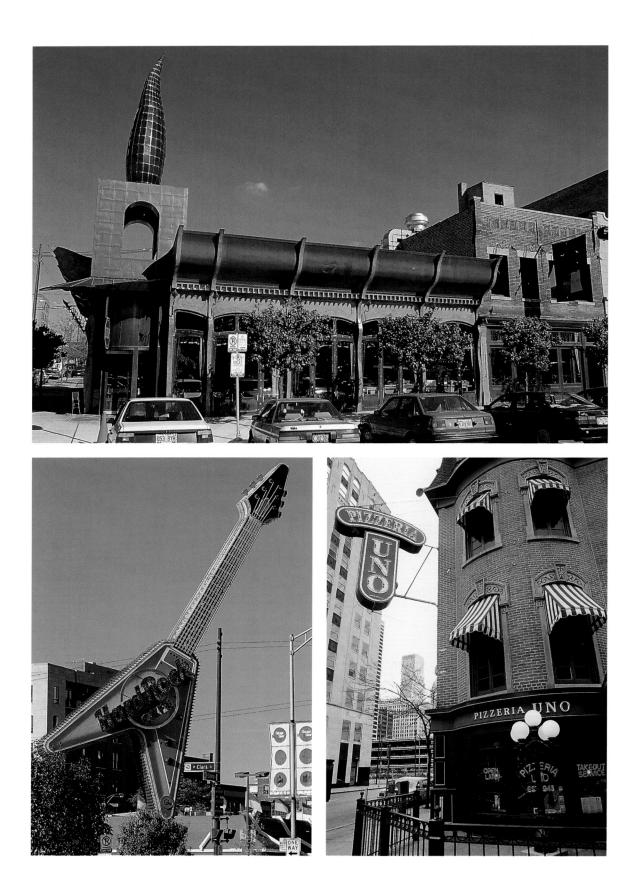

(top) The Redlight Chinese restaurant, in Chicago's Market District.

(bottom left) The Hard Rock Cafe, in River North.

(bottom right) Pizzeria Uno—Chicagoans are passionate about their pizza.

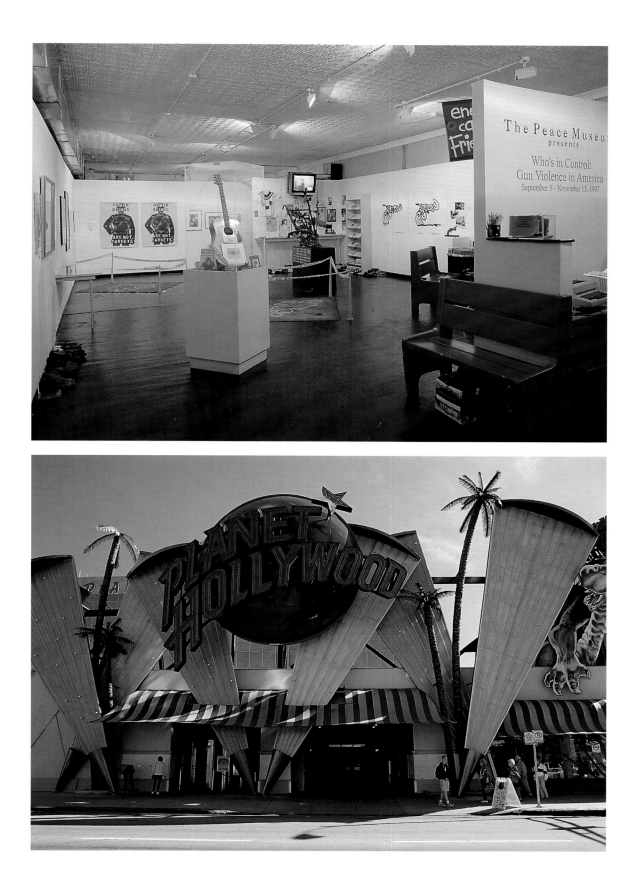

(top) The Peace Museum, River North, offers four exhibits per year dedicated to world peace.

(bottom) Chicago's Planet Hollywood.

(overleaf) The Chicago River skyline at sundown.

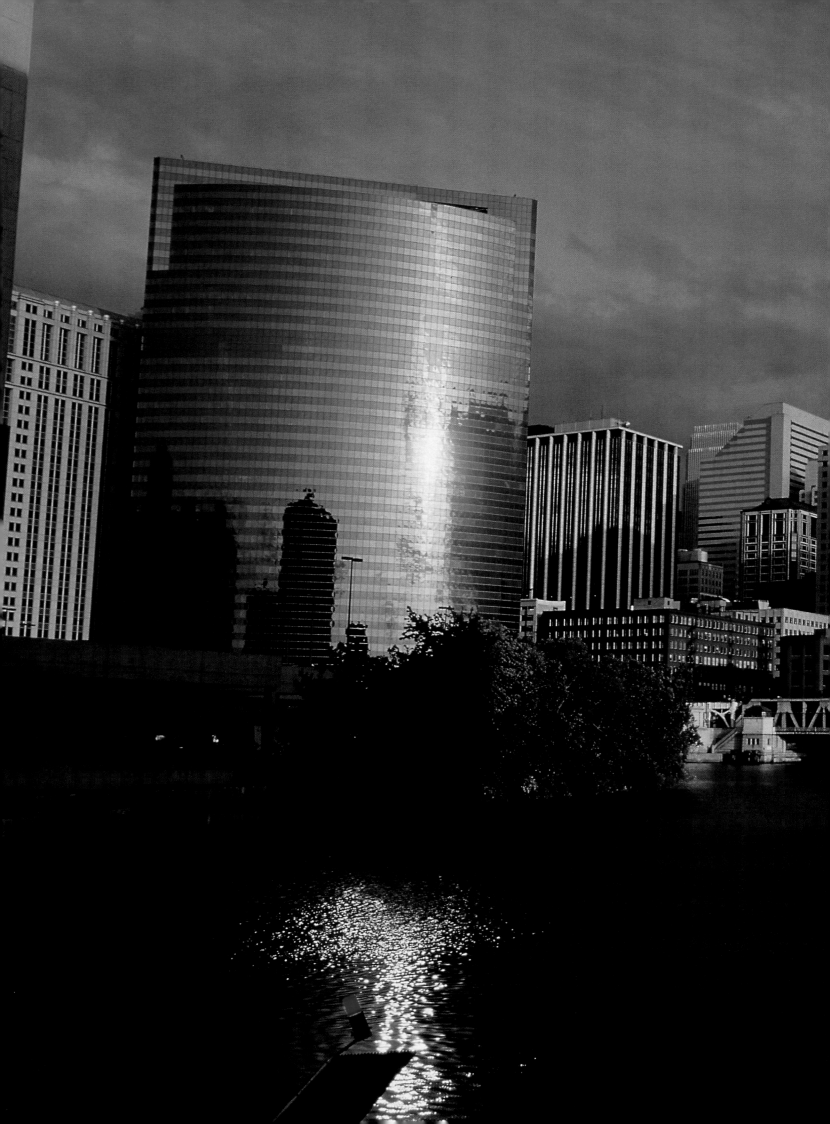

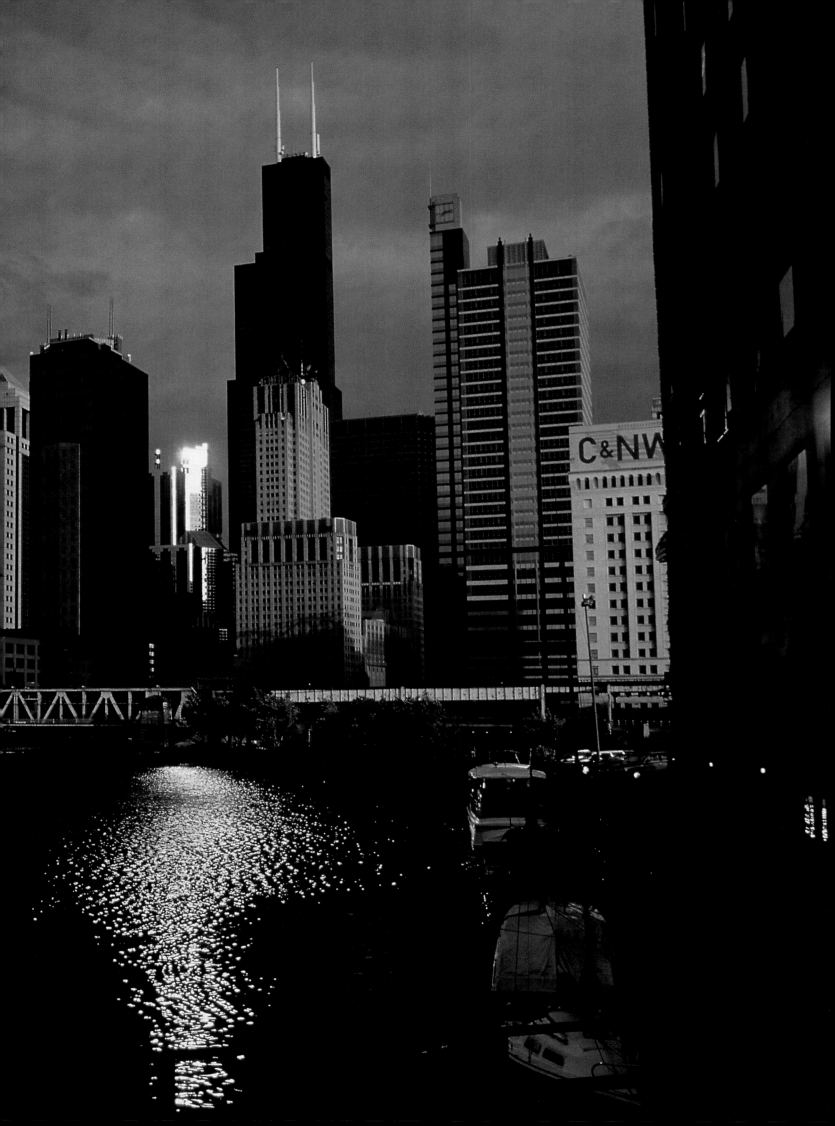

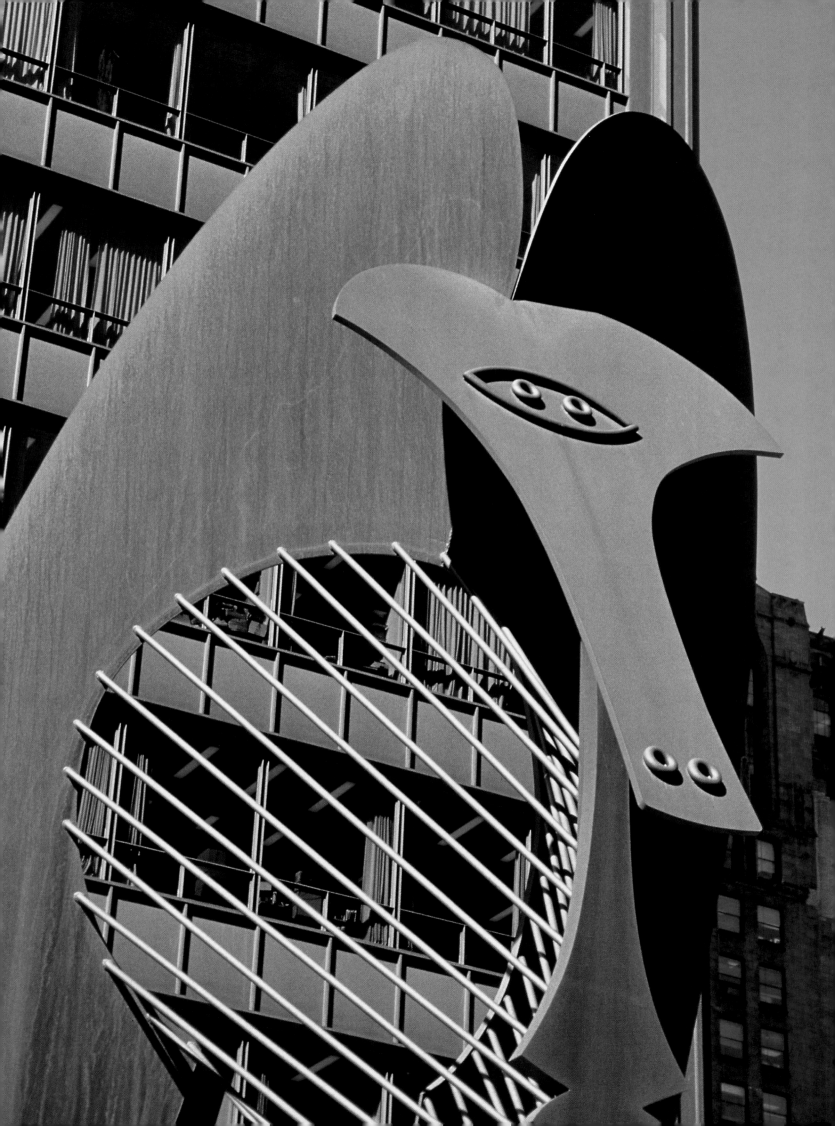

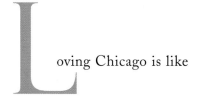

oving Chicago is like

loving a woman with a broken nose."

—Nelson Algren

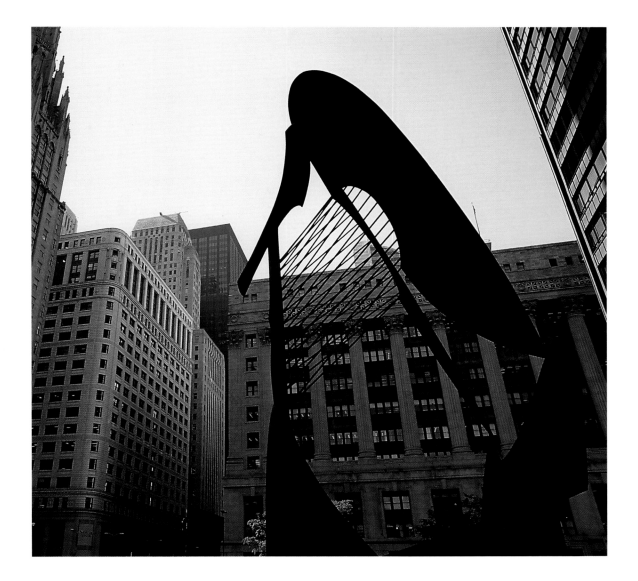

(above and left) In the Daly Center Plaza sits an untitled sculpture by Pablo Picasso. Usually referred to as "The Chicago Picasso," this Cor-Ten steel sculpture was unveiled in 1967.

(overleaf) The Sears Tower dominates the city skyline dramatically at night.

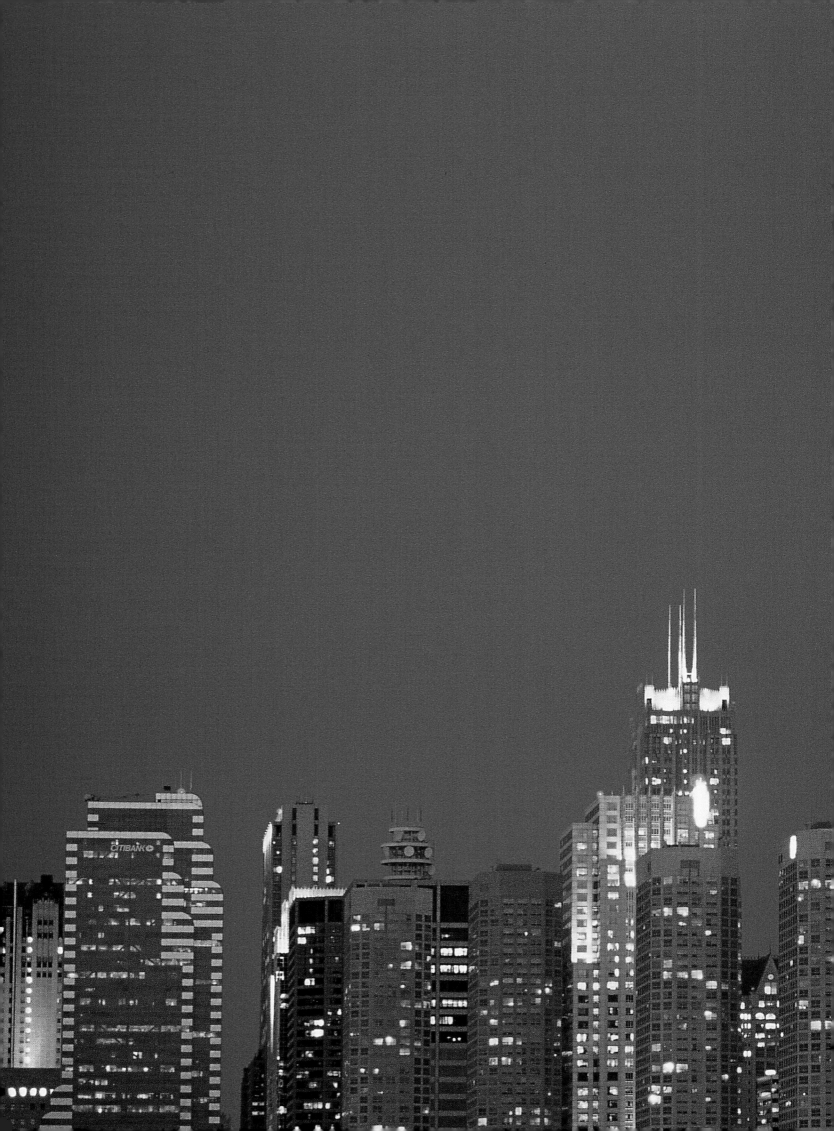

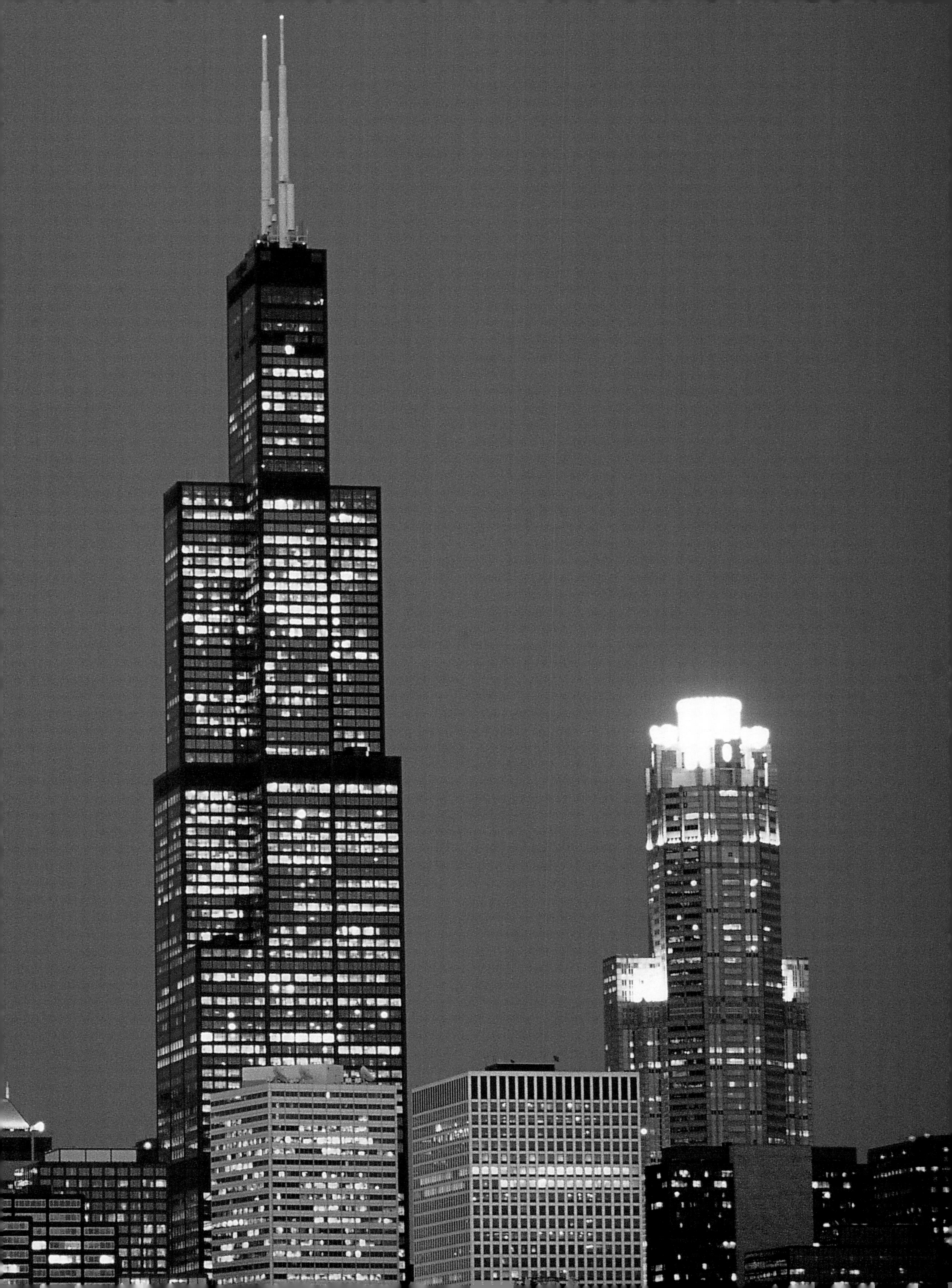

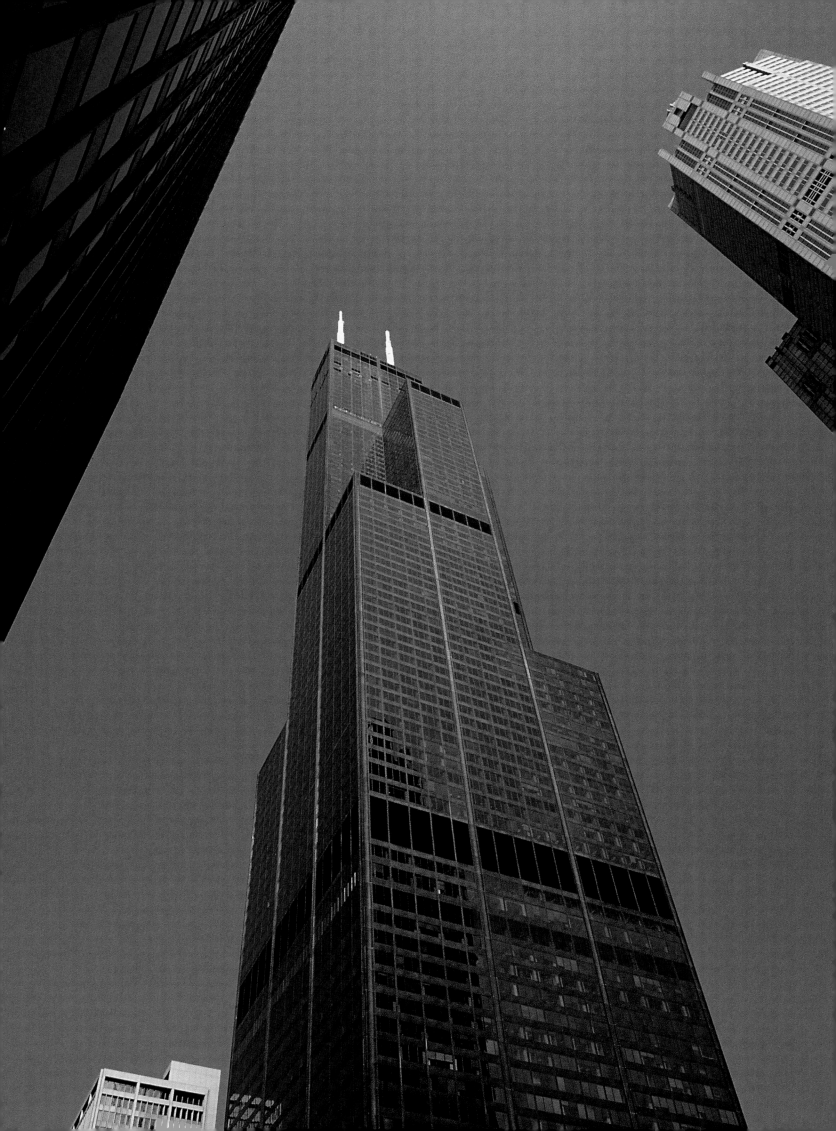

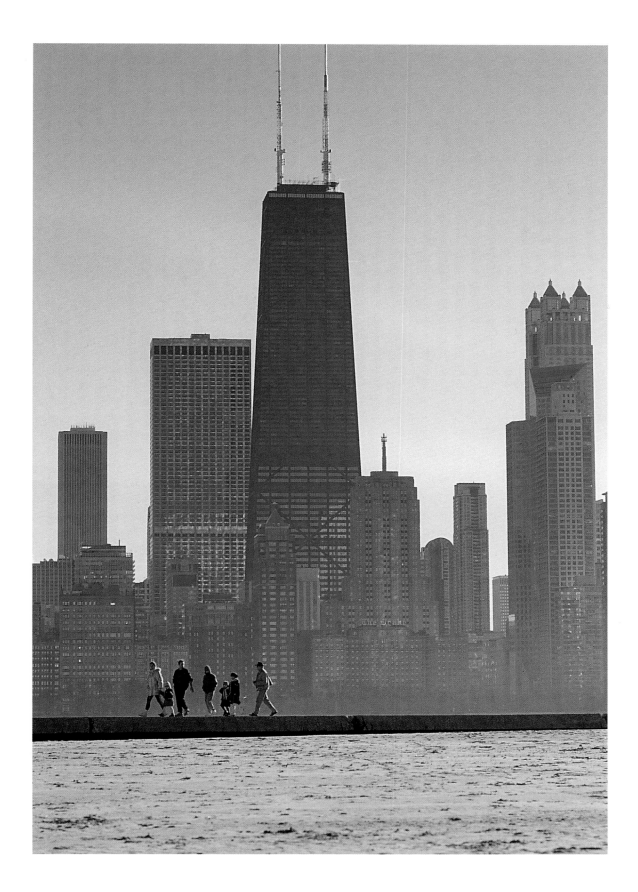

(left) The 110-story Sears Tower was designed by Skidmore, Owings & Merrill and built in 1973. It features a skydeck 1,450 feet up, on the 103rd floor. It was the world's tallest building until 1996 and regained the tallest building title in 1997.

(above) The John Hancock building from the waterfront.

(overleaf) High-rise office buildings line Wacker Drive along the riverfront.

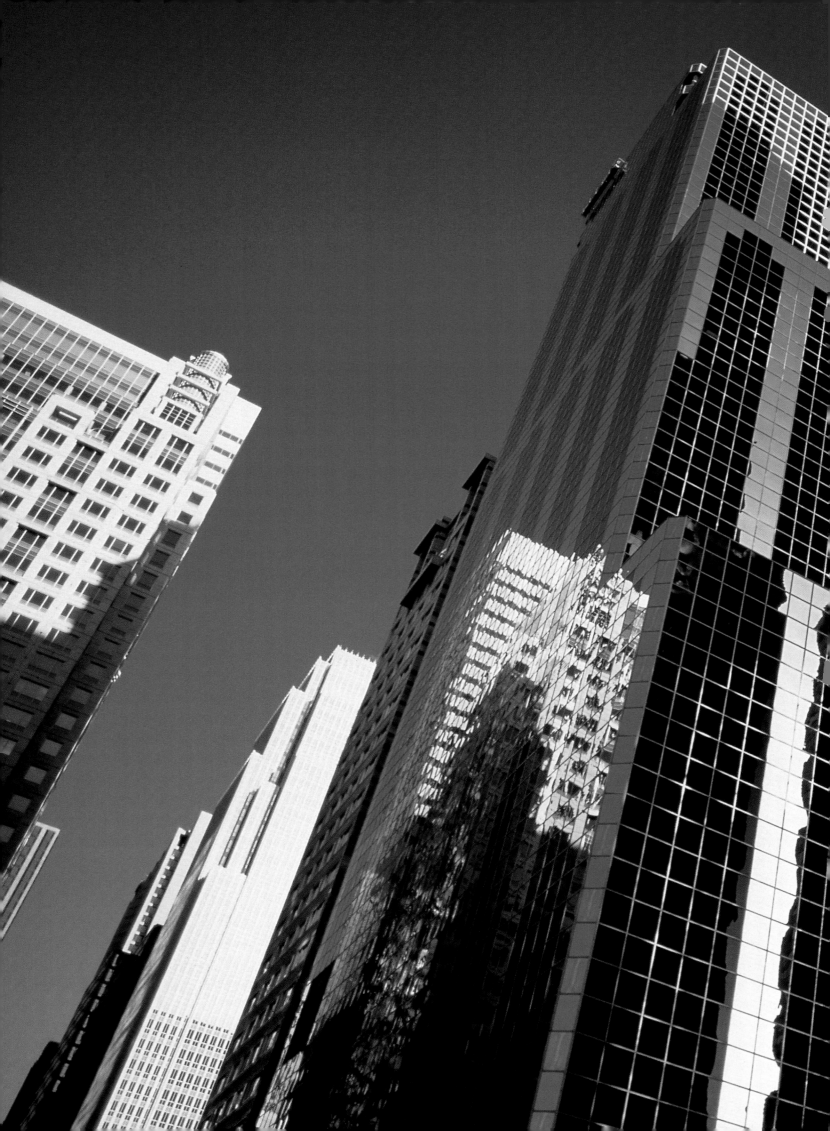

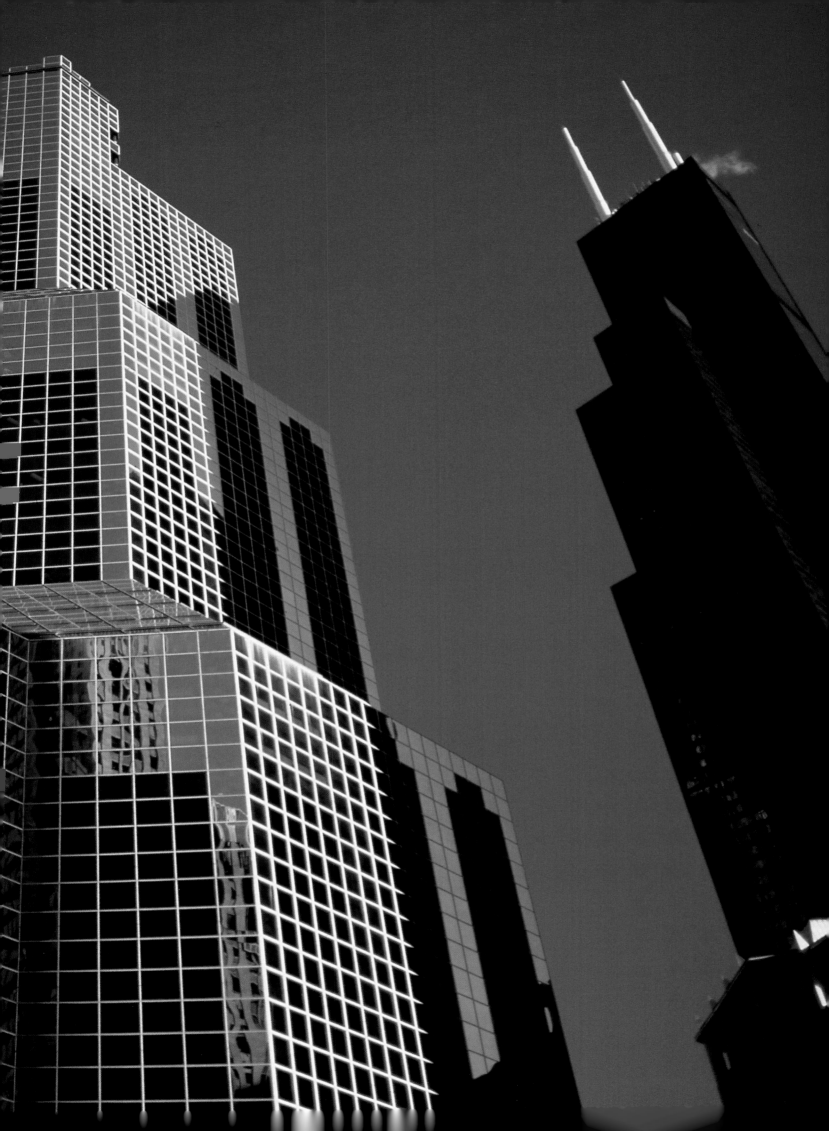

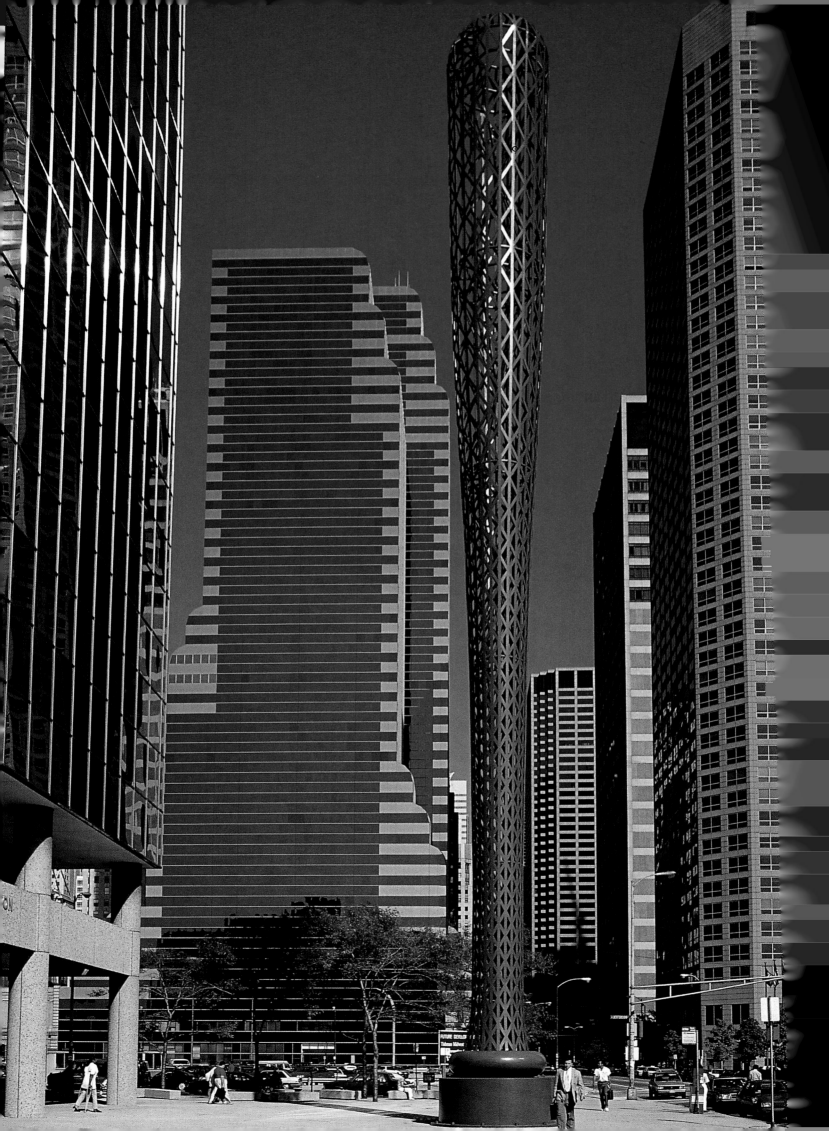

There's a freshness, a vitality about the city.

It hasn't been corroded with ultra-sophistication

and with its citizens' esteeming of their own quality.

Yet at the same time it's a magnificent city

—the architecture, the music.

It's enough to make your mouth drop open."

—Gerald Arpino

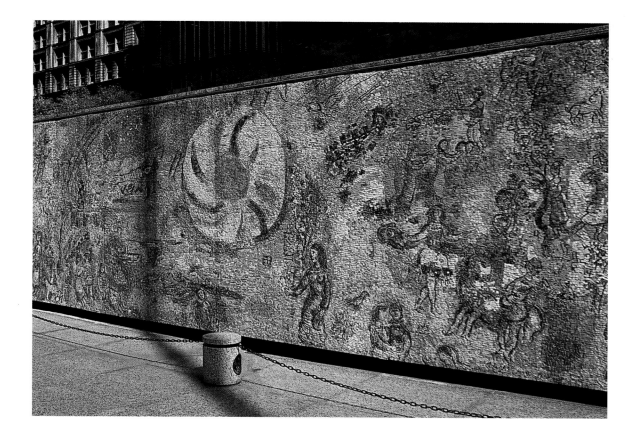

(left) This 101-foot-high steel baseball bat, "The Batcolumn," is a 1977 sculpture by Claes Oldenburg.

(above and overleaf) "The Four Seasons," Marc Chagall's 1974 mosaic mural, is made up of thousands of hand-chipped stone and glass fragments in more than 250 colors. The entire mosaic spans 4,000 square feet.

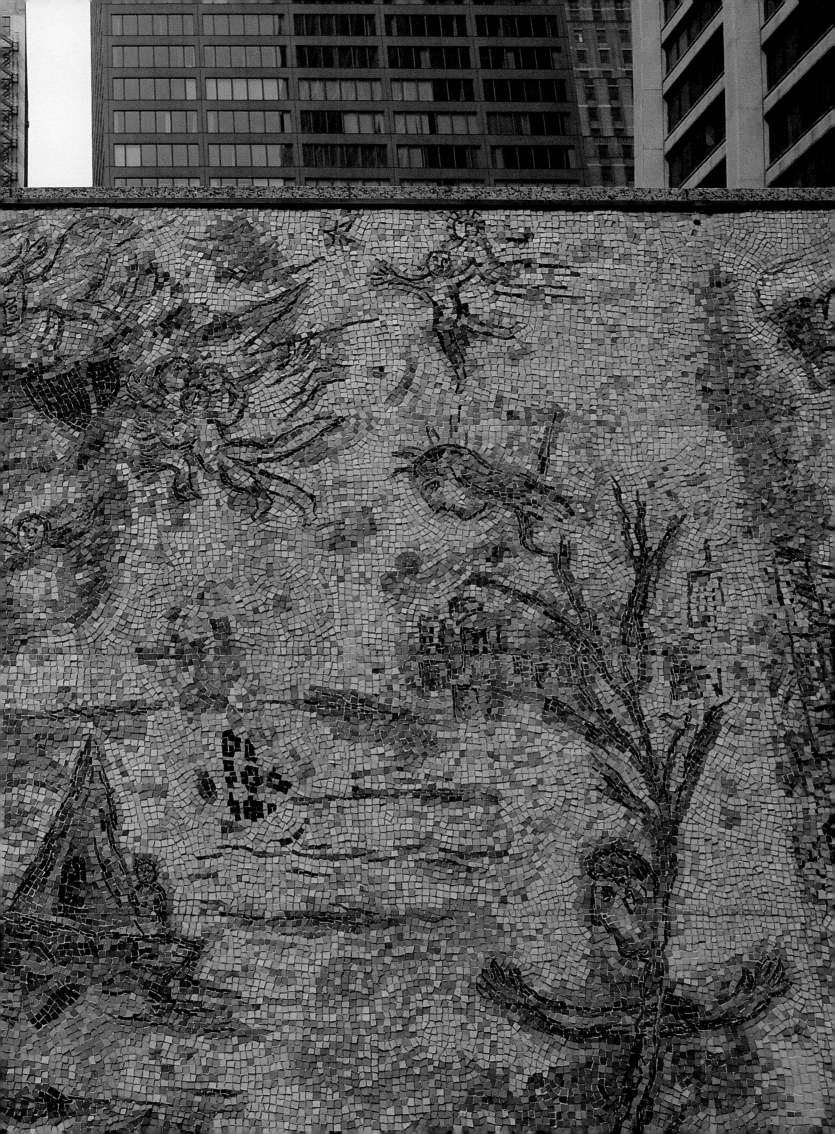

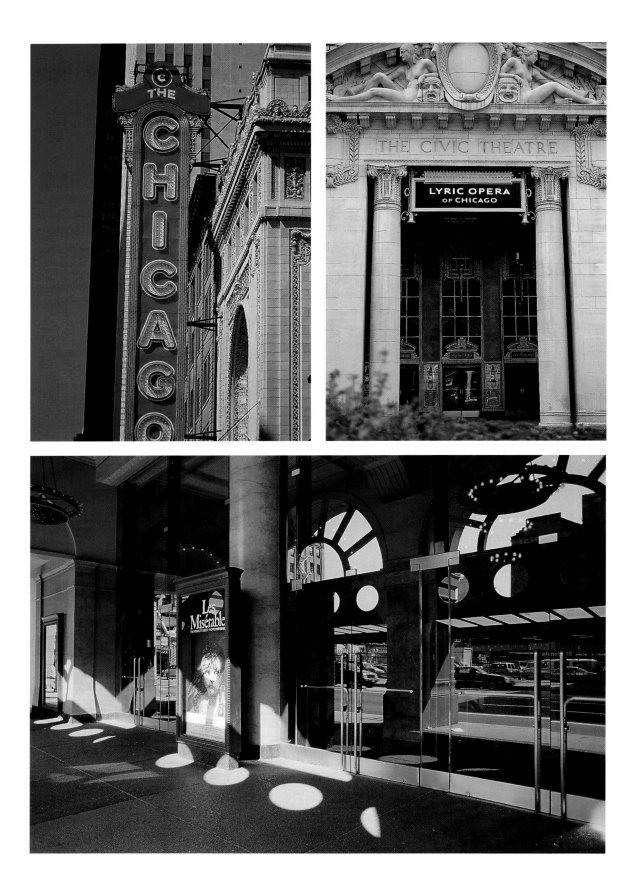

(top left) State Street's Chicago Theater. **(top right)** Chicago Civic Opera House. **(bottom)** Auditorium Theater.

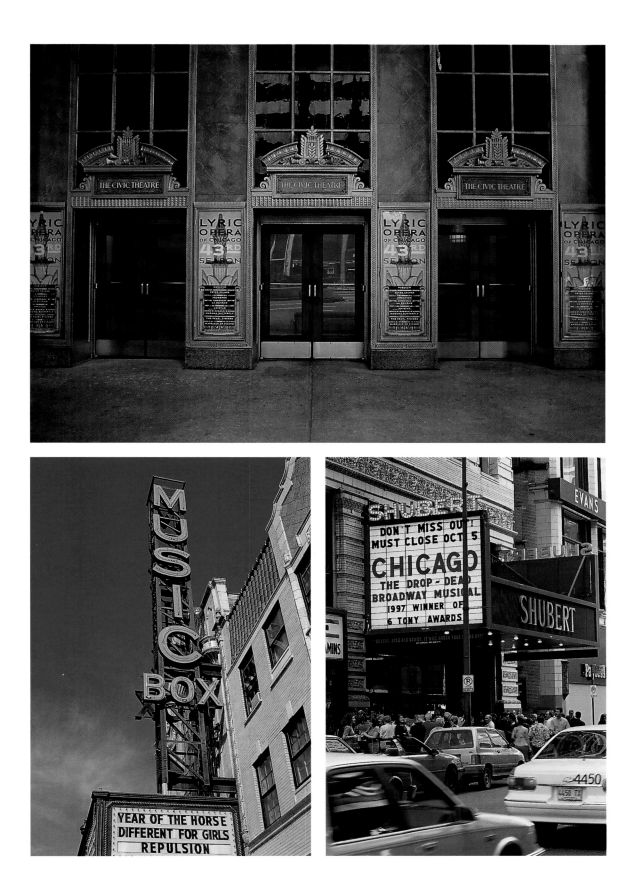

(top) Chicago Civic Opera House. (bottom left) Music Box Theater. (bottom right) Shubert Theater.

(overleaf) Chicago Board of Trade building and Art Deco clock.

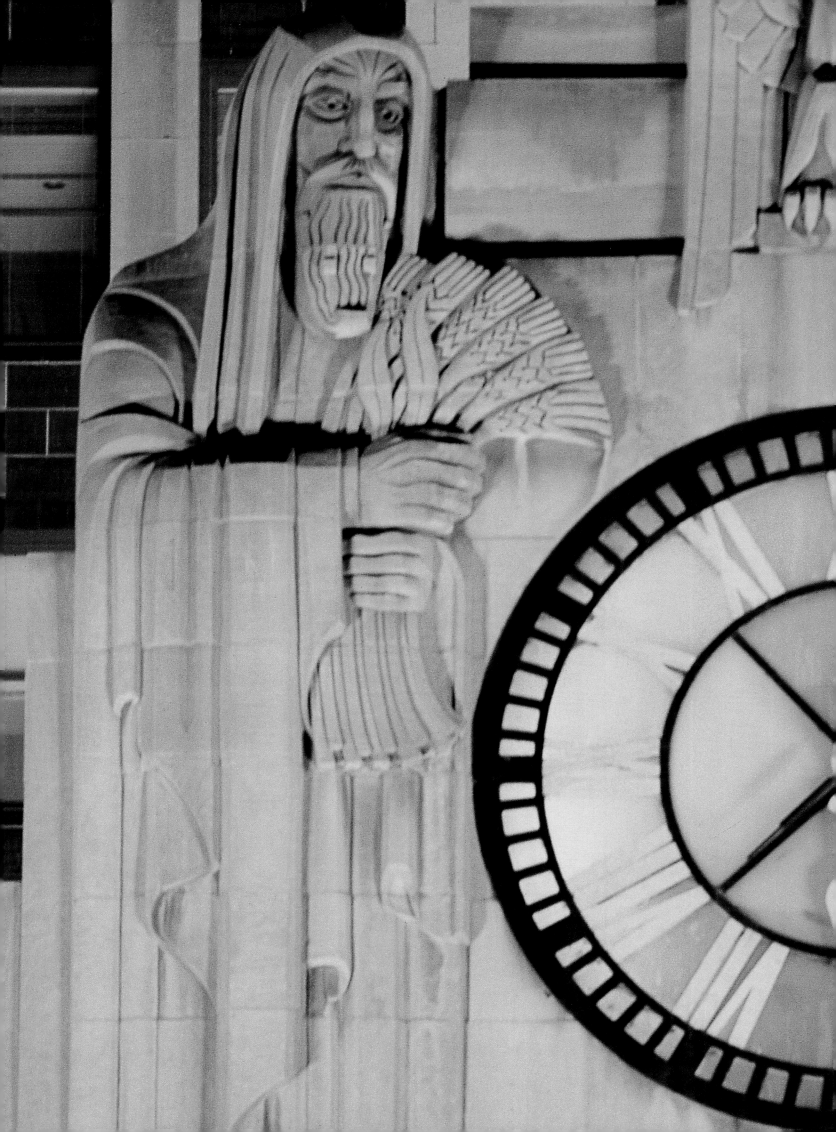

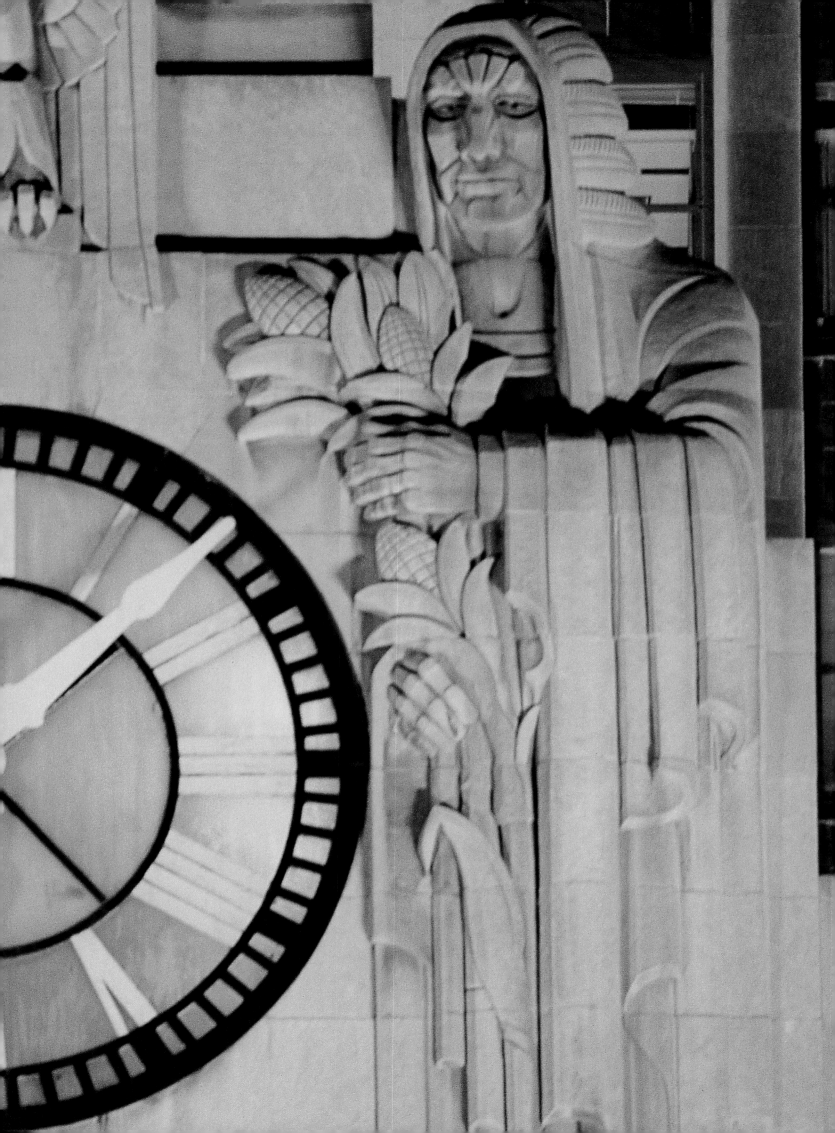

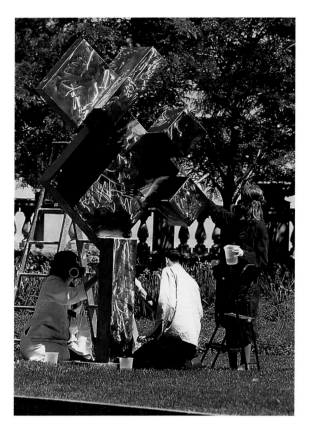

C

hicago is one of those cities

we feel we know a lot about because

it has such a prominent place

in the imaginative life

of the twentieth century. . . ."

—Salman Rushdie

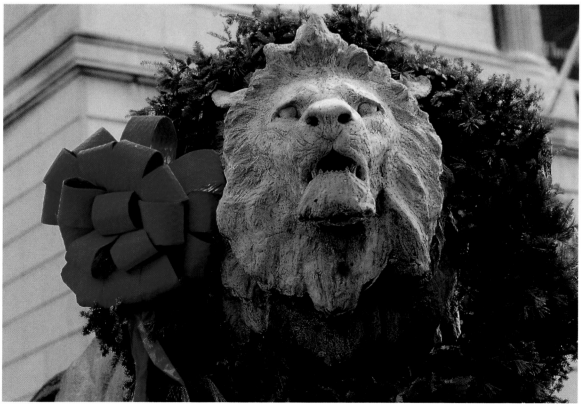

(top) Students at the Art Institute of Chicago.

(bottom) One of two bronze lions guarding the entrance to the Art Institute.

(right) A view up Michigan Avenue from the gardens of the Art Institute.

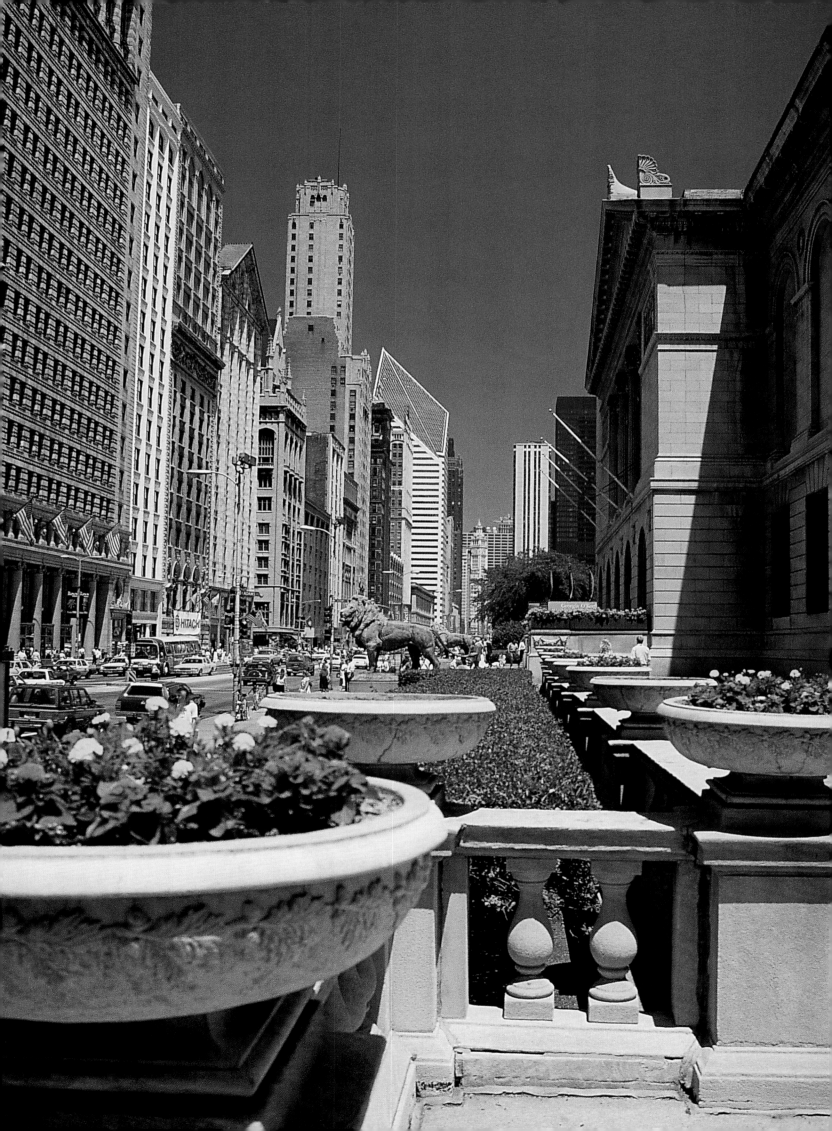

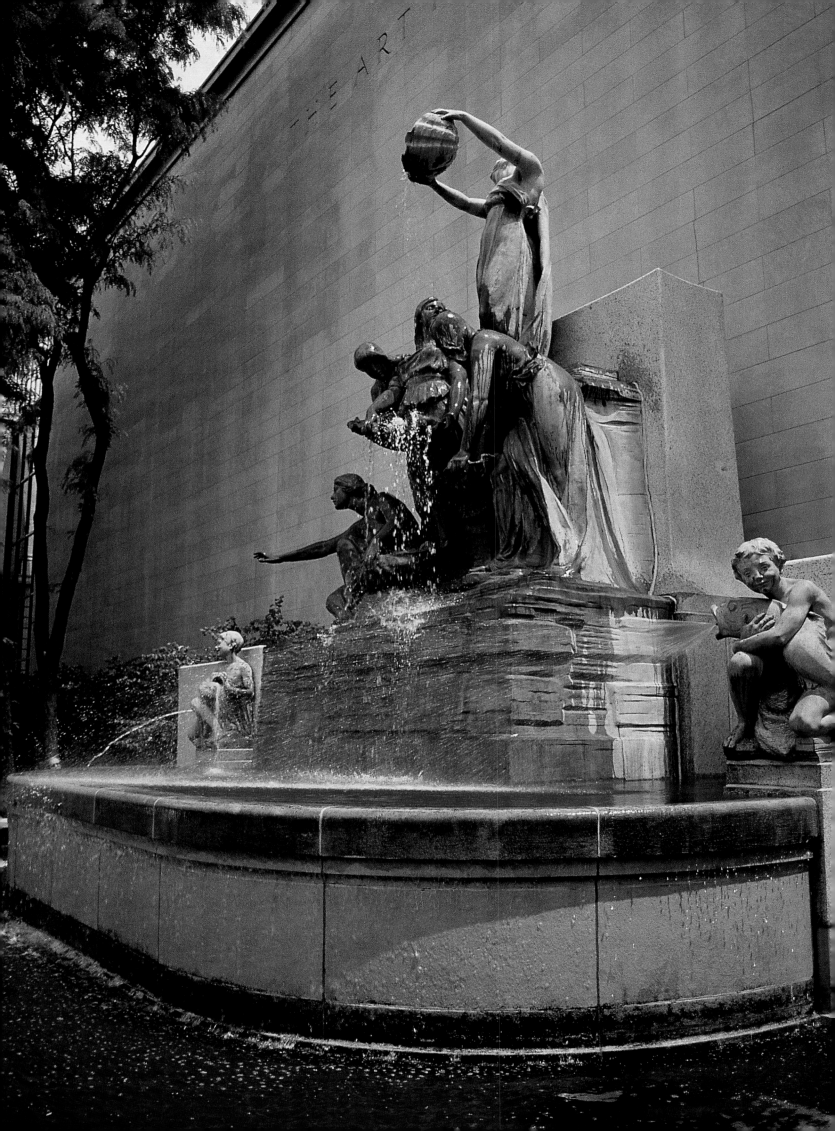

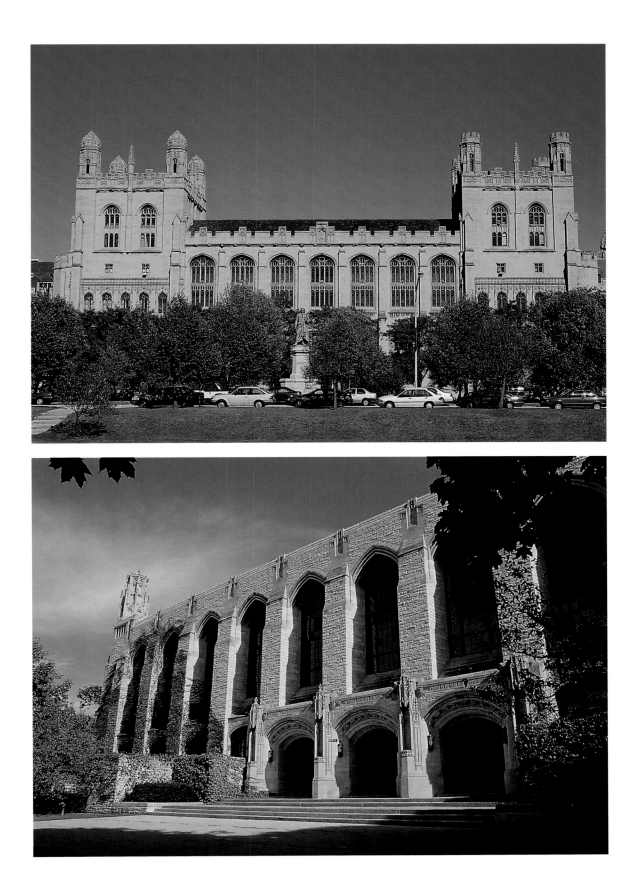

(left) Sculpture at the Art Institute. **(top)** The University of Chicago. **(bottom)** Northwestern University, Evanston.

(overleaf) The spectacular, illuminated Tiffany dome atop Preston Bradley Hall in the Chicago Cultural Center.

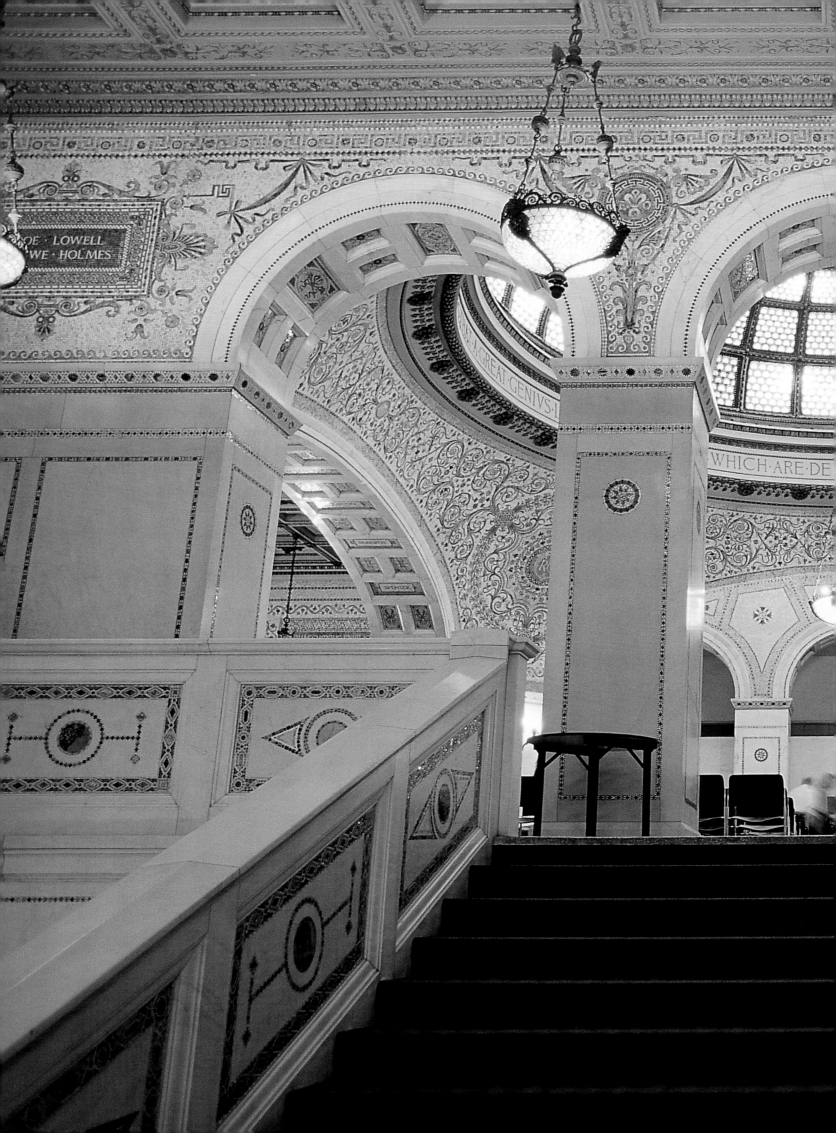

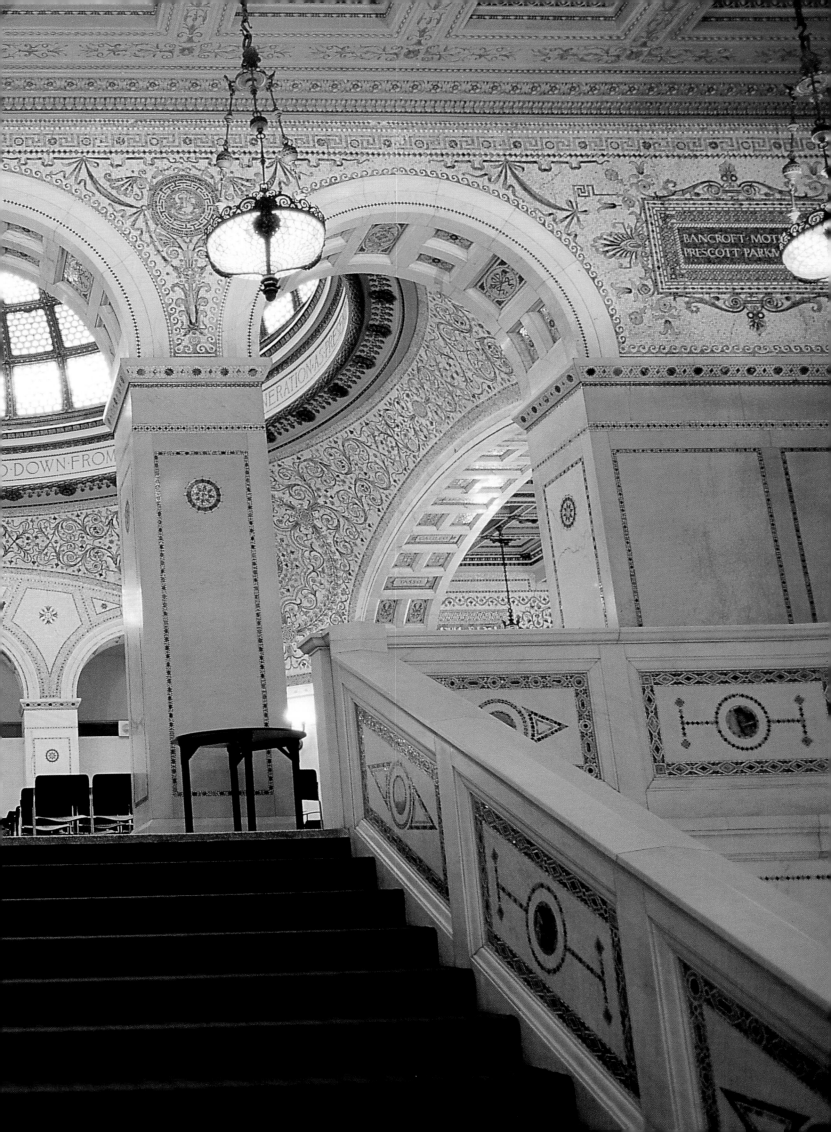

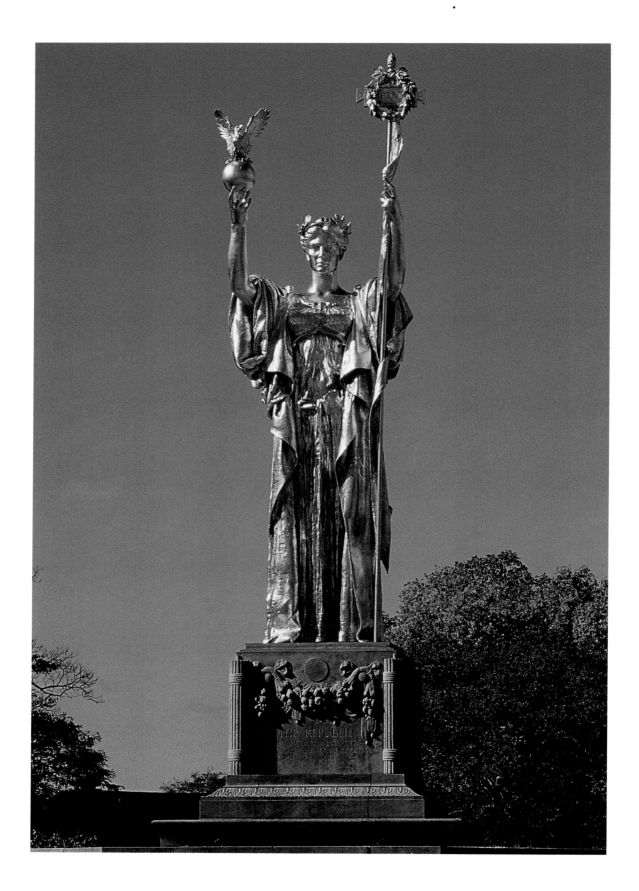

(above) The Republic Statue was erected in 1918 for the Chicago World's Fair.

(right) Buckingham Fountain with Sears Tower in the background.

(overleaf) Buckingham Fountain at night.

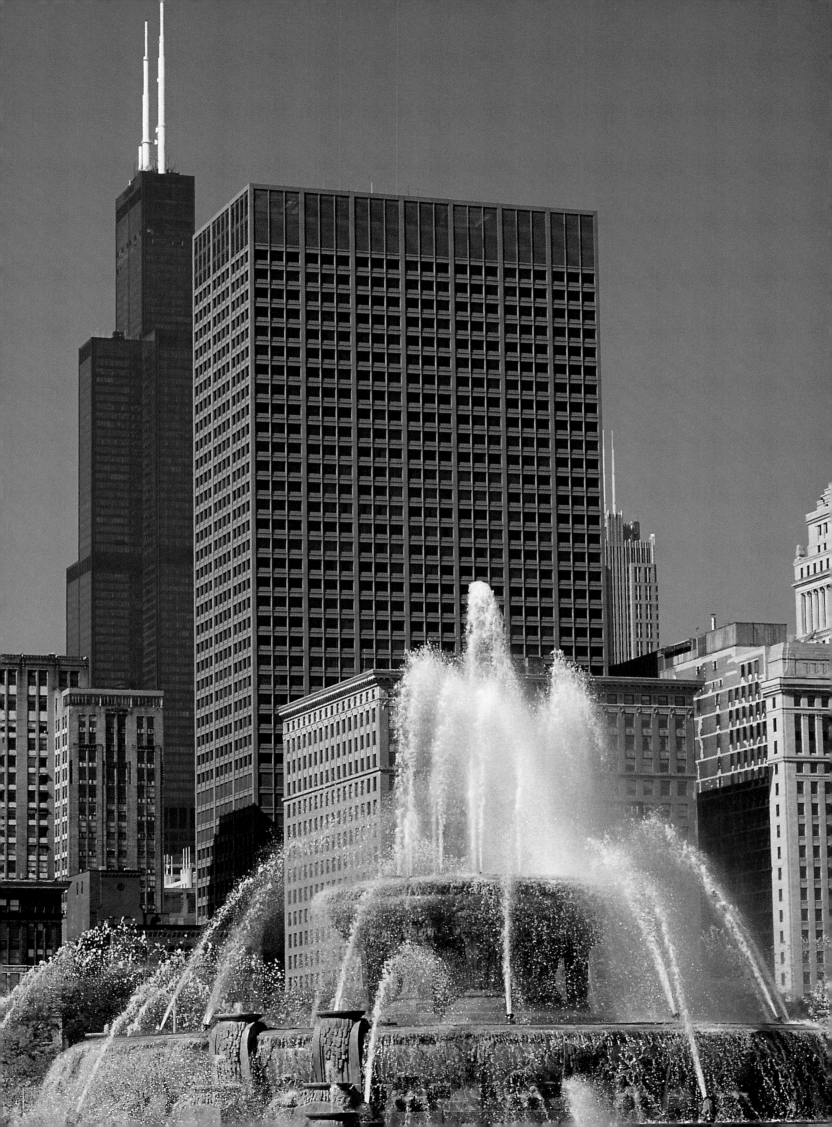

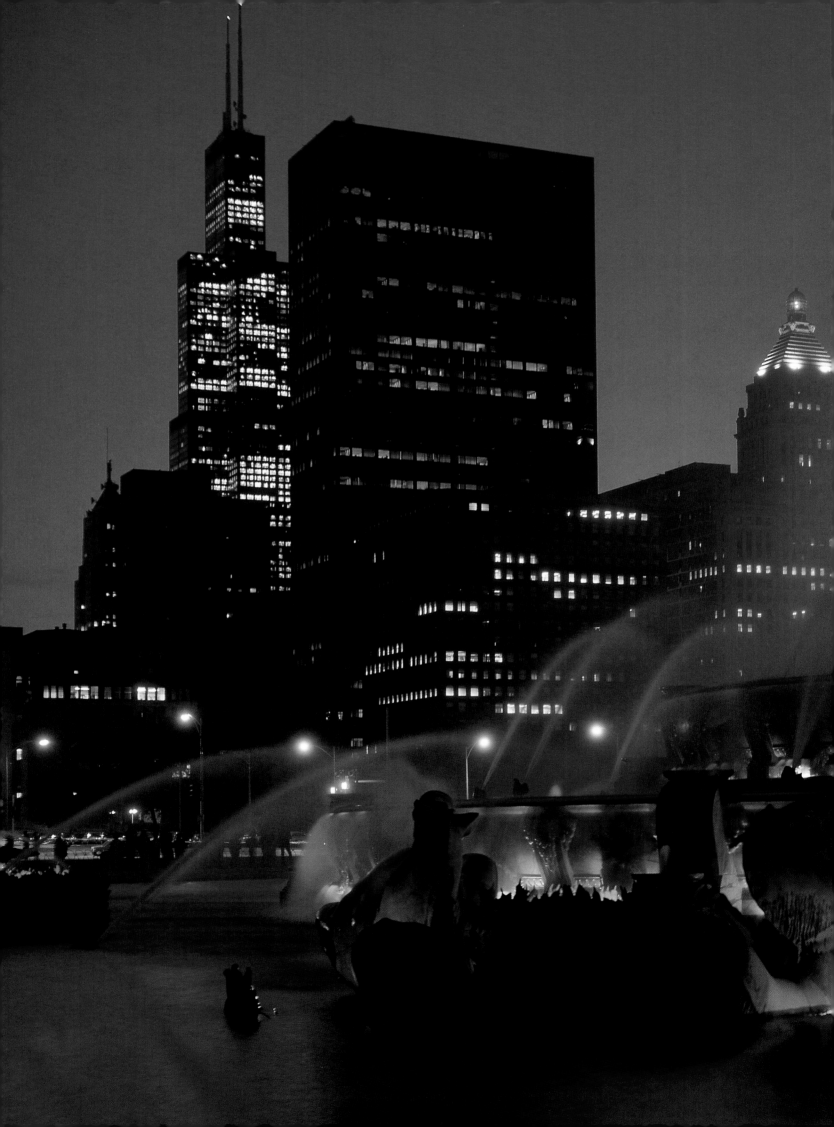

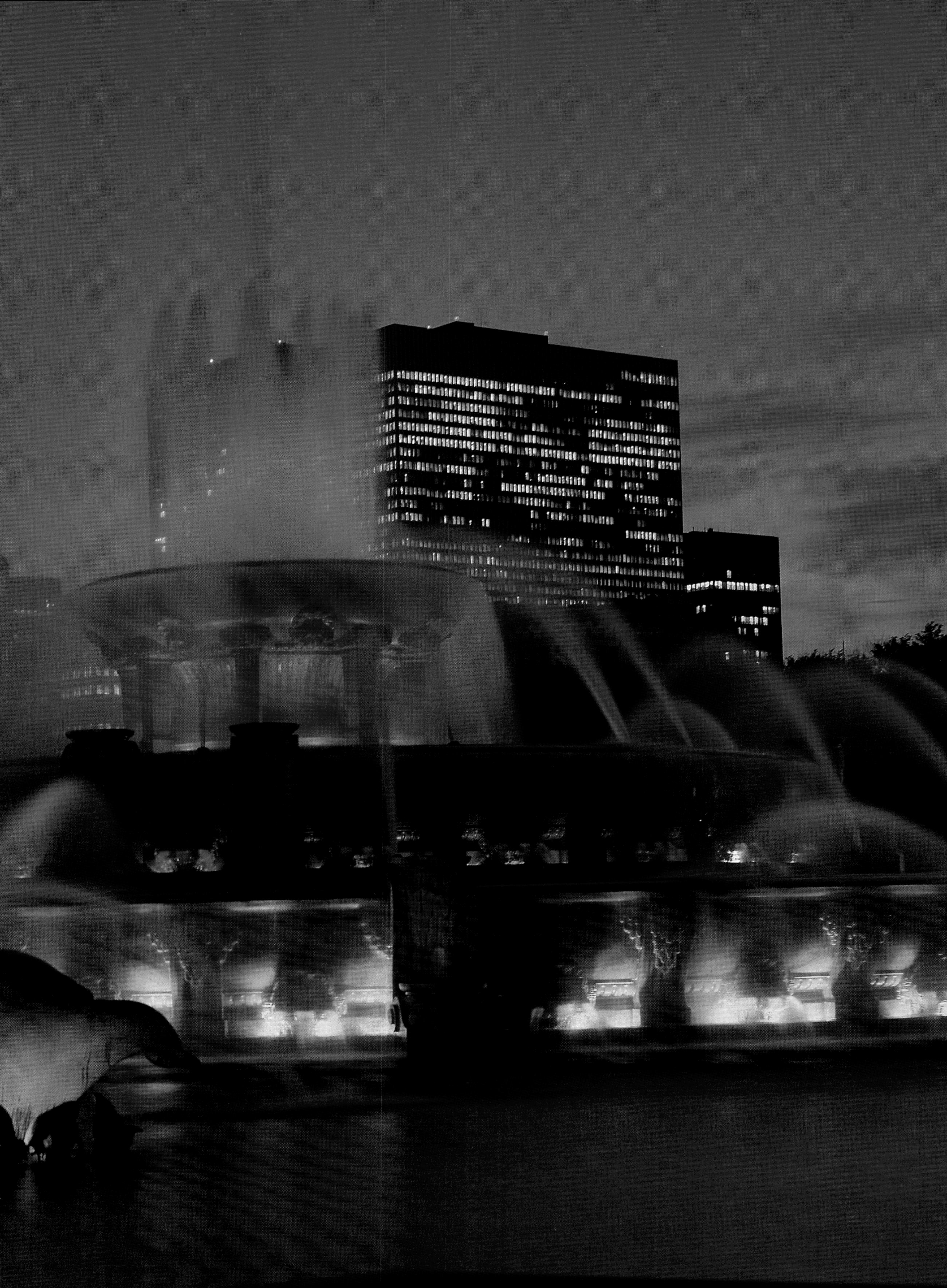

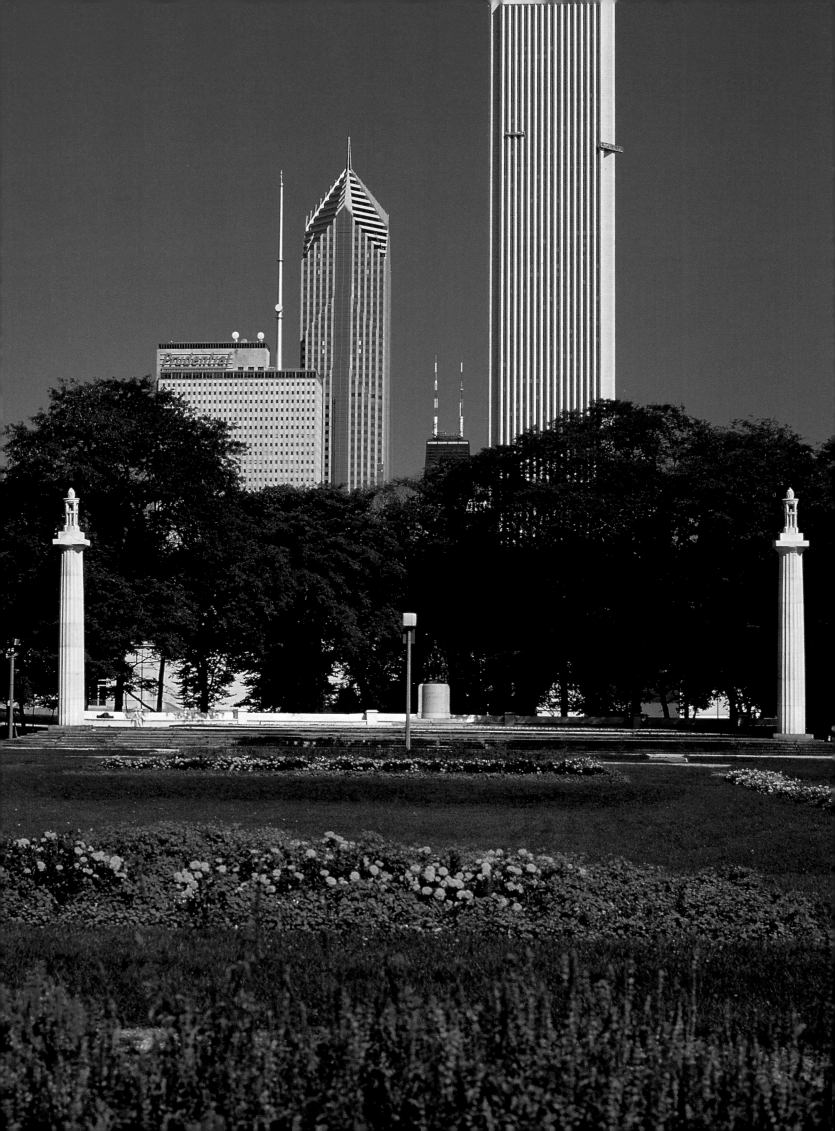

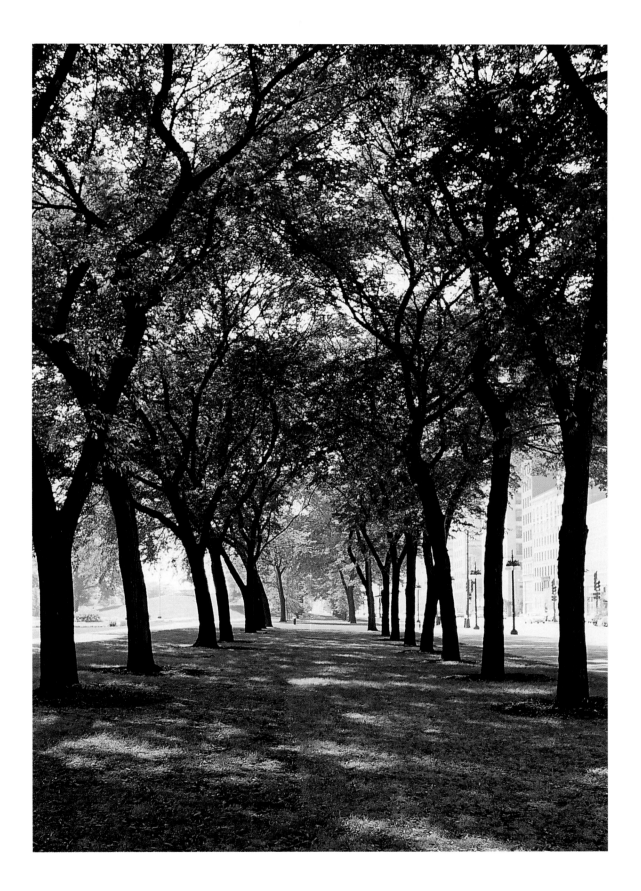

(left, above, and overleaf) Grant Park.

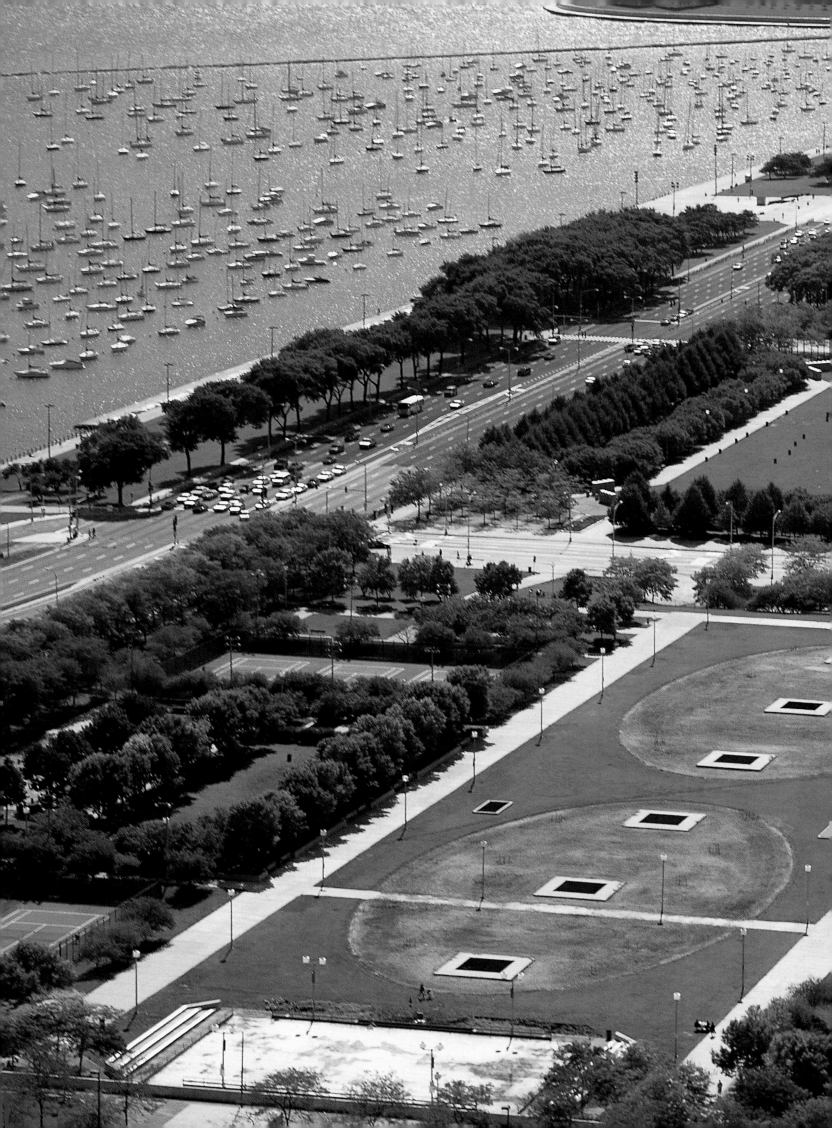

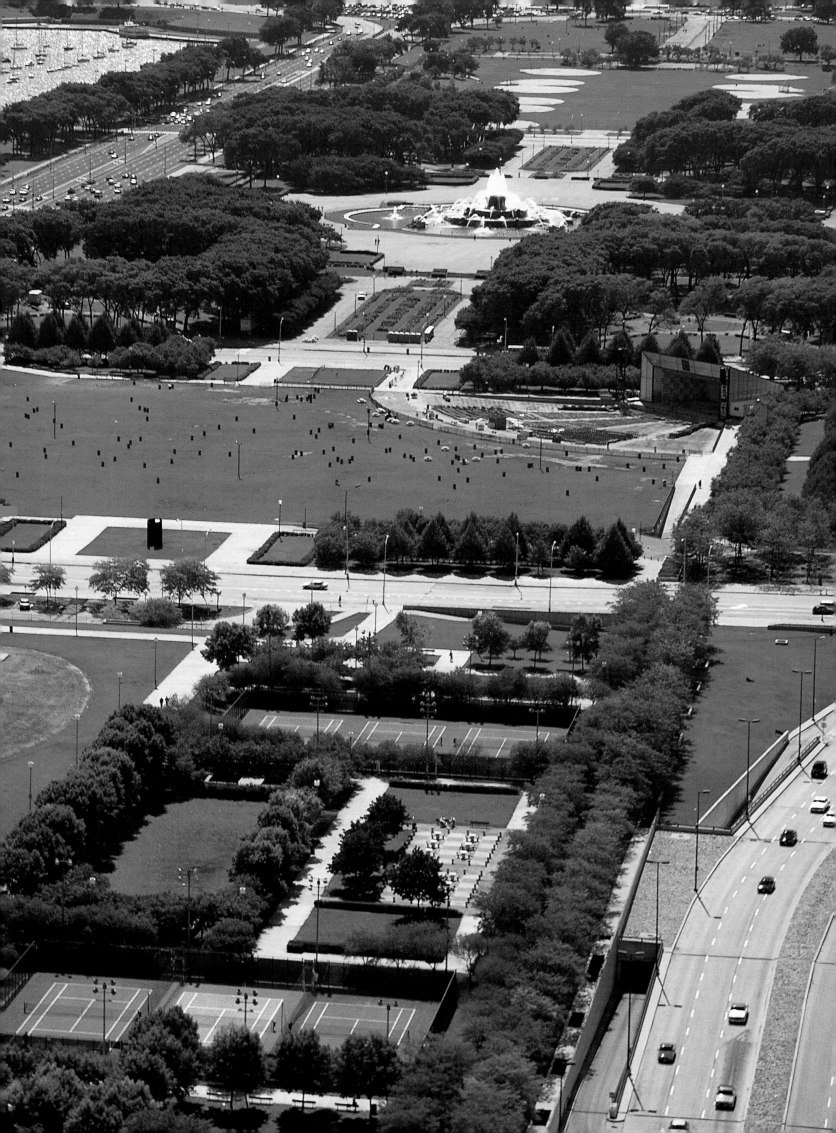

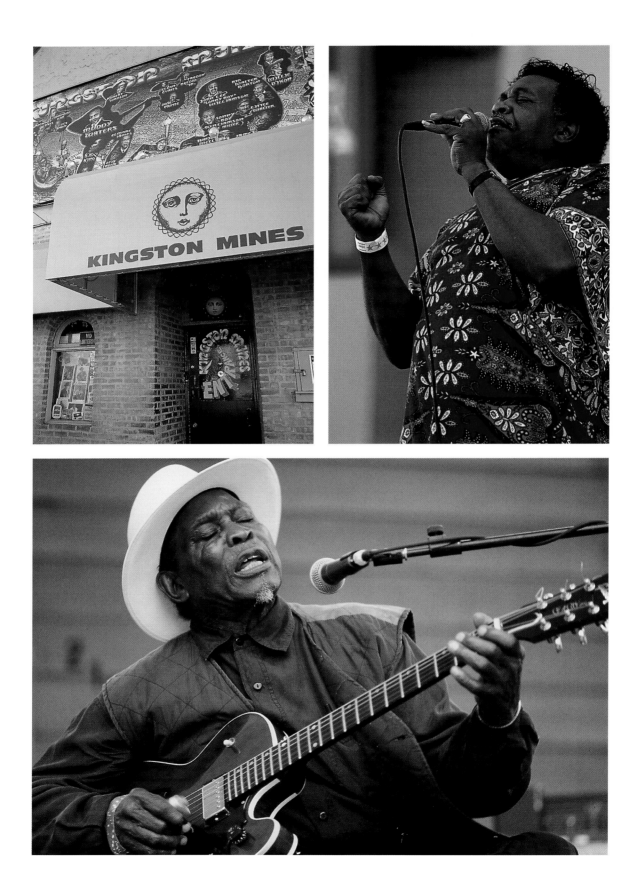

(top left) Kingston Mines Blues Club.

(top right) Martin Albritton at the Chicago Blues Fest, held every summer in Grant Park.

(bottom) David Honeyboy Edwards at the Chicago Blues Fest.

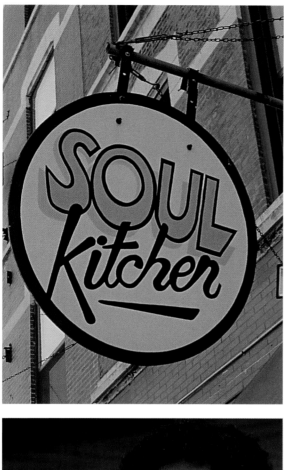

H ad I known in 1890 how long

it would take me to preserve

a park for the people against their will,

I doubt if I would have undertaken it."

—Aaron Montgomery Ward

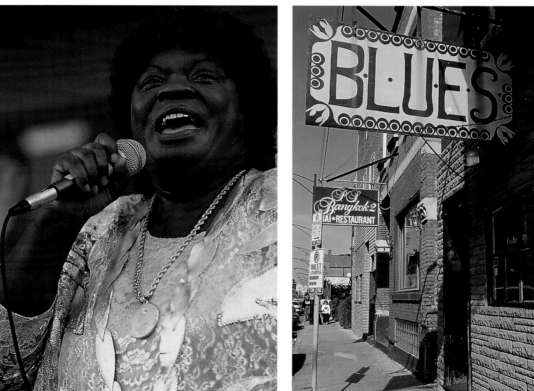

(top) Soul Kitchen Restaurant, Wicker Park.

(bottom left) Koko Taylor at the Chicago Blues Fest.

(bottom right) Chicago Blues Club, Lincoln Park.

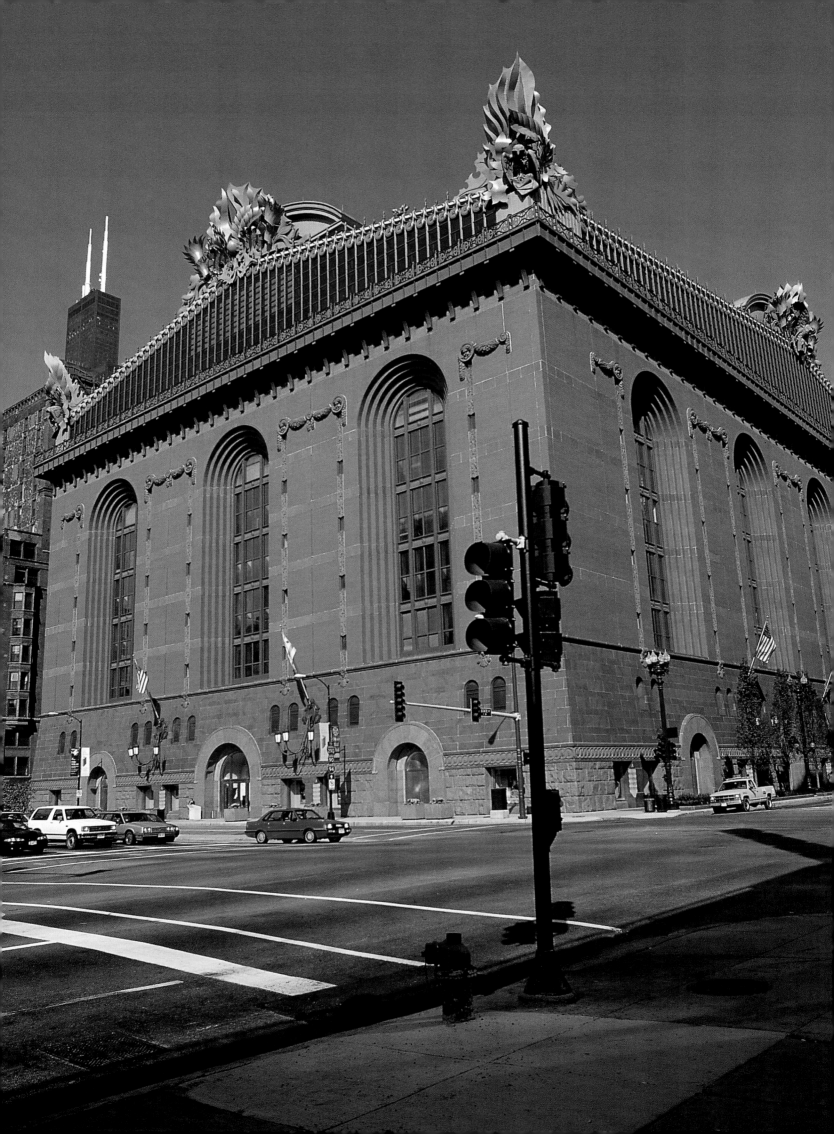

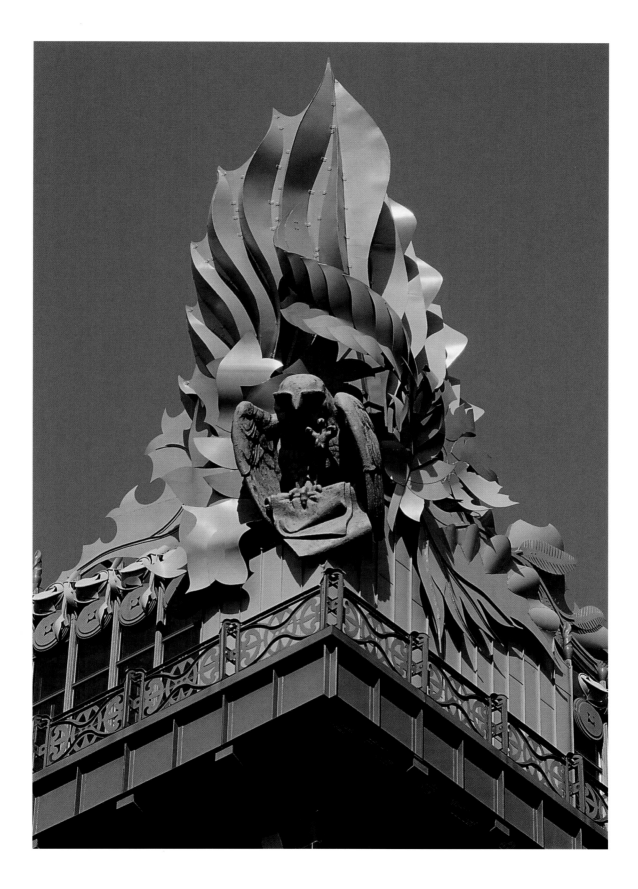

(above and left) Harold Washington Library Center.

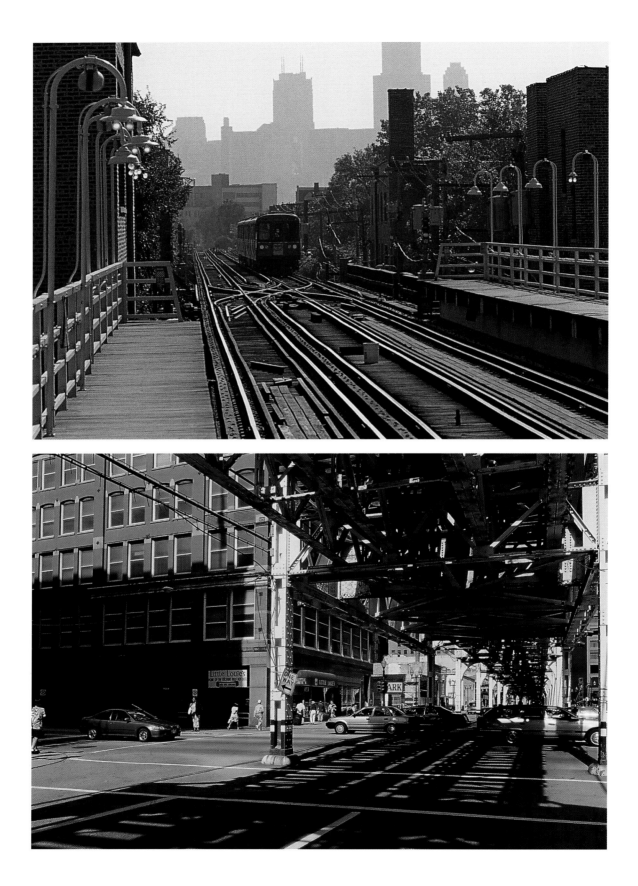

(top) Chicago's "el" trains are a throwback to another era but still provide a vital link in the city's public transportation system.

(bottom) Beneath the el.

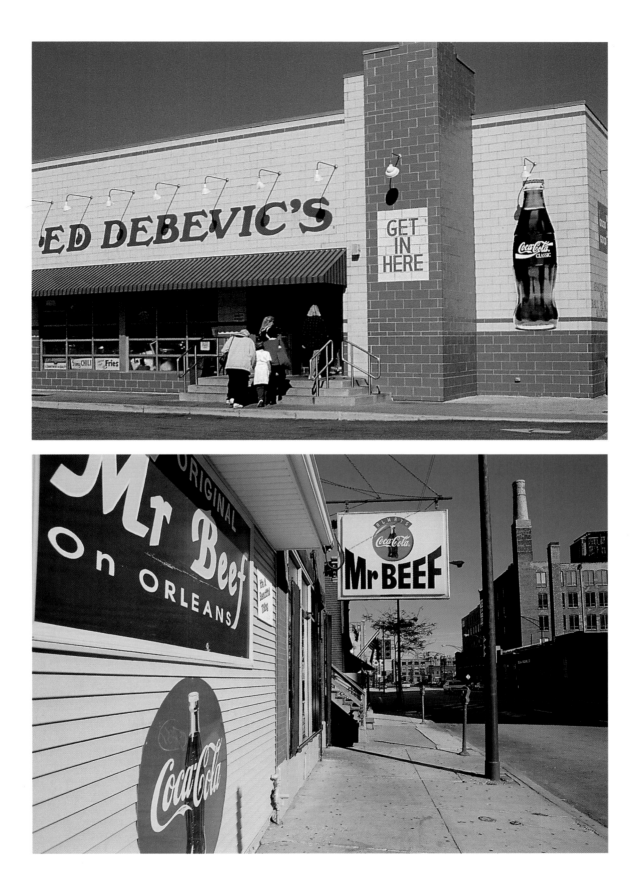

(top) Ed Debevic's restaurant evokes the spirit of the 1950s.

(bottom) Even Jay Leno eats at Mr. Beef, a sandwich joint in the River North area.

(overleaf) Downtown at night.

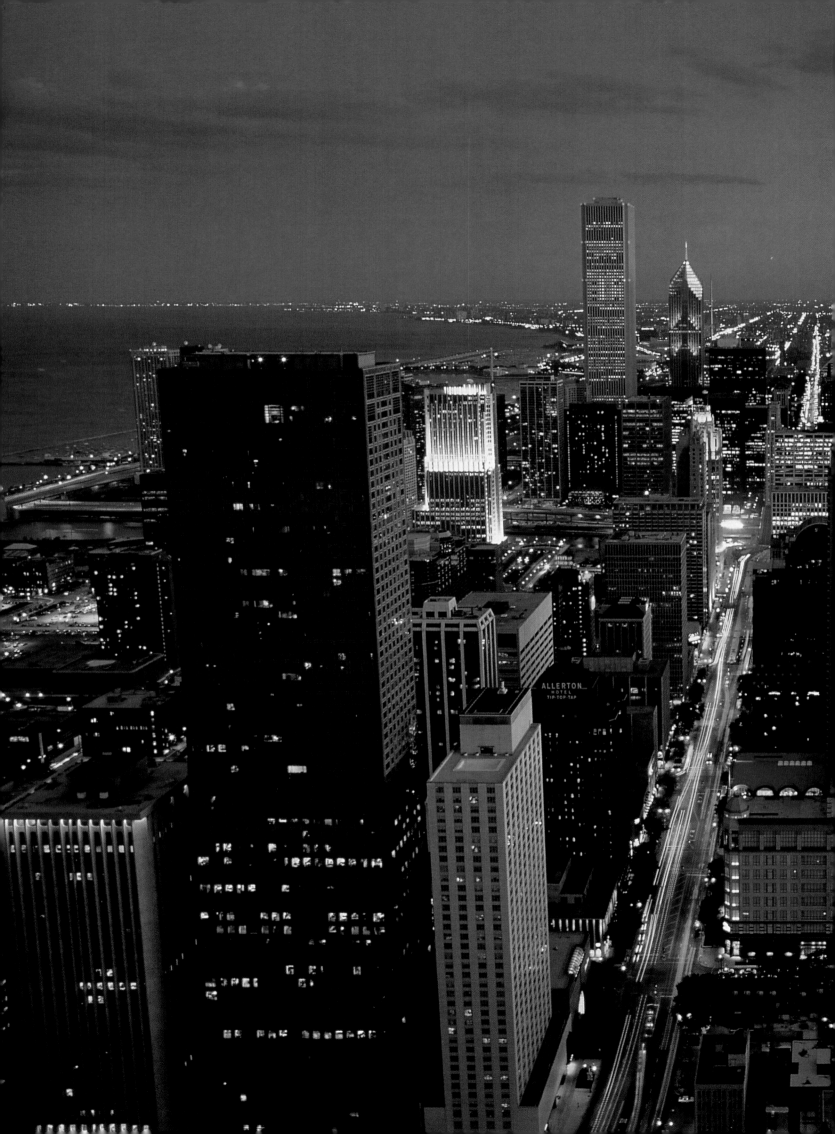

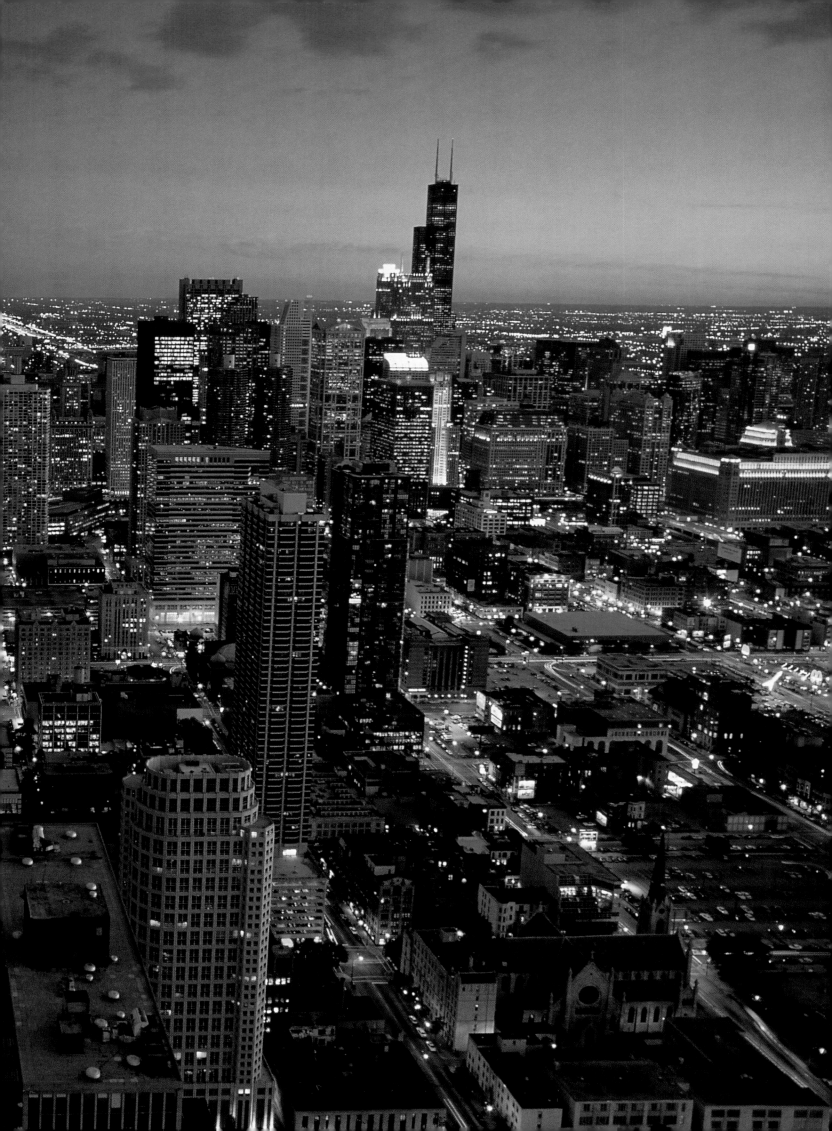

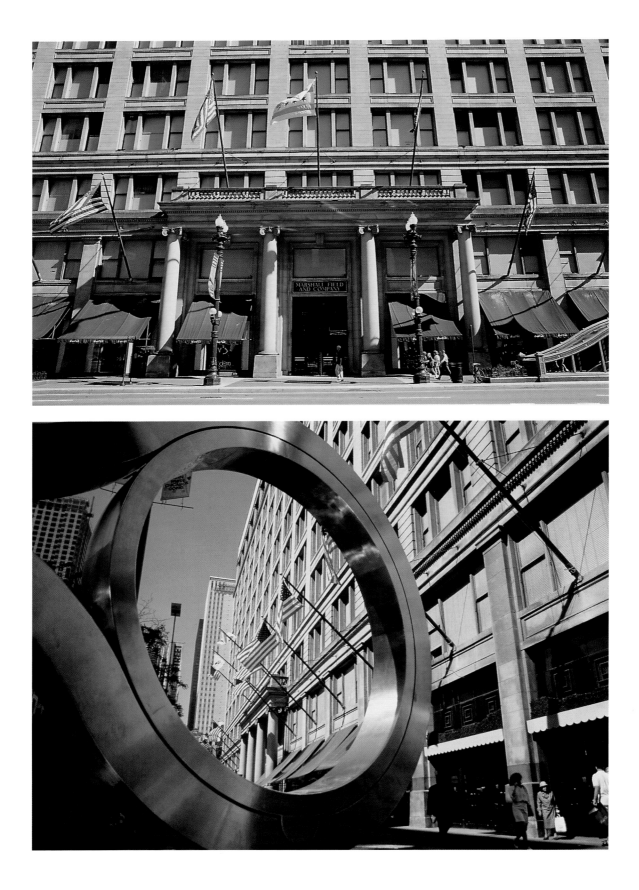

(top) Marshall Field's department store on State Street.

(bottom) A stainless steel sculpture by Virginia Ferarri, "Being Born," pays homage to the tool and die industry.

(right) Christmas on State Street.

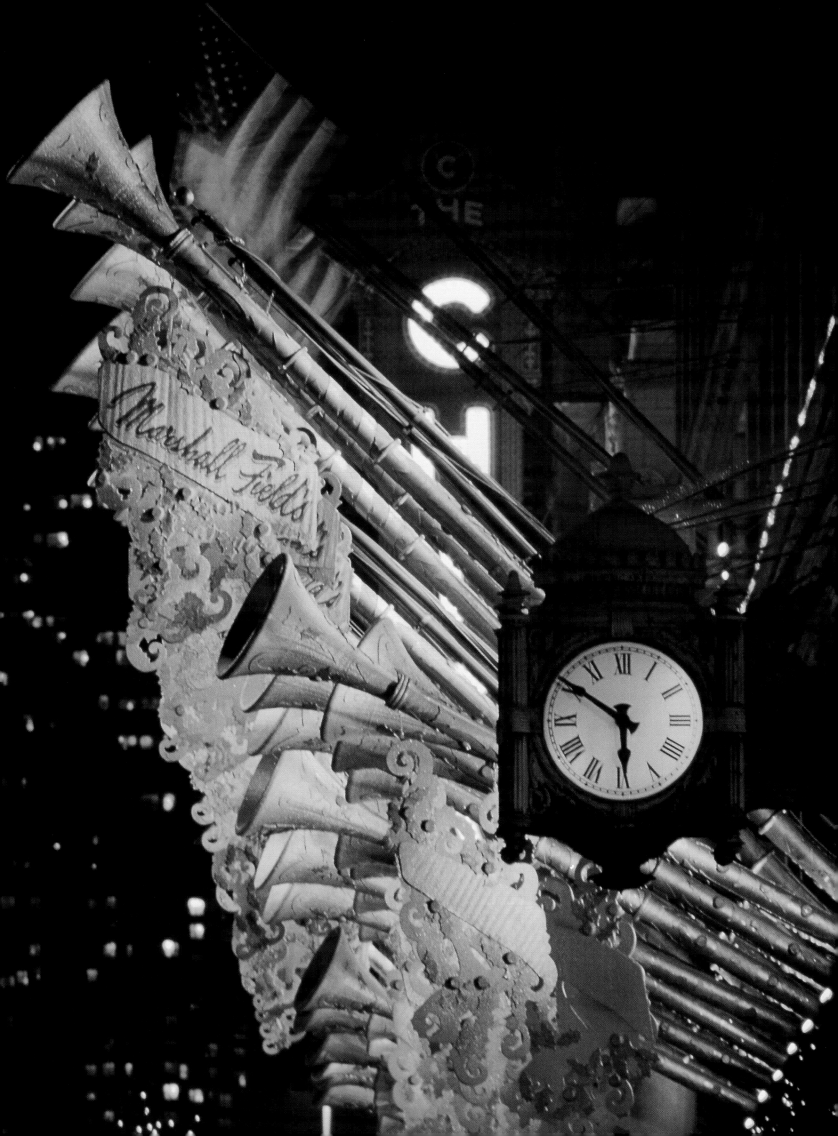

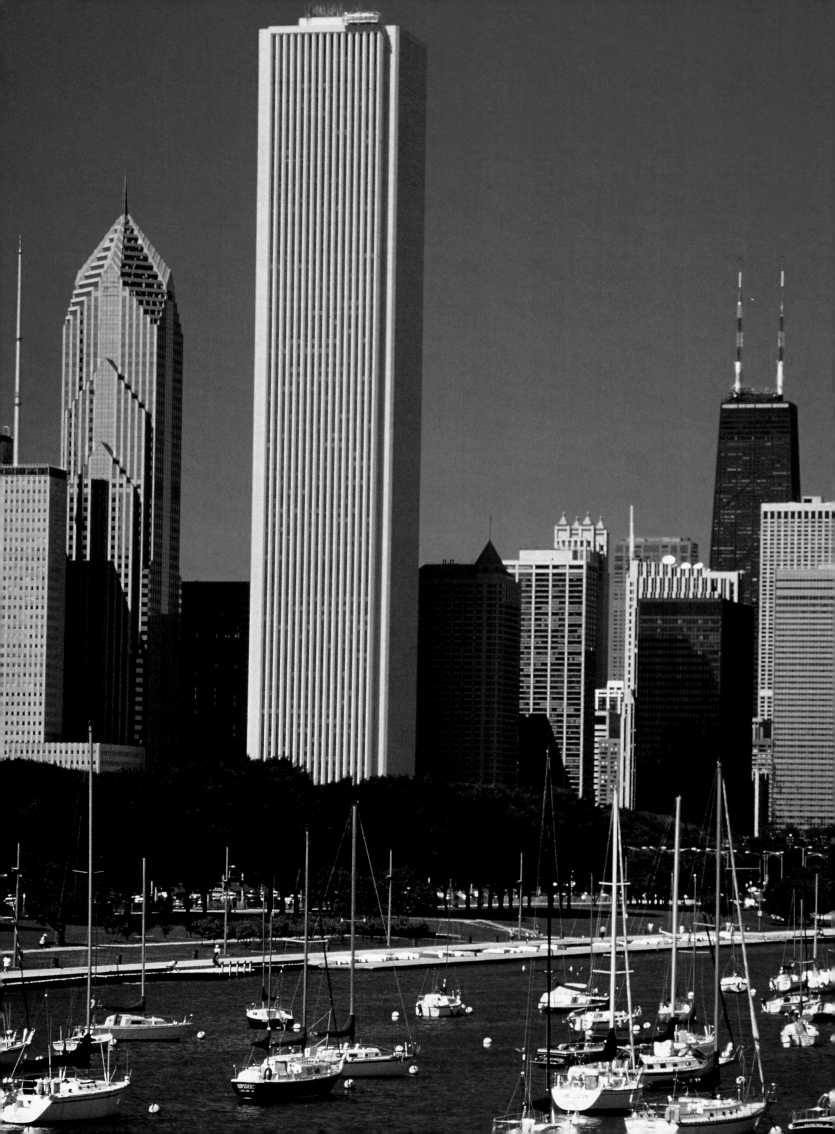

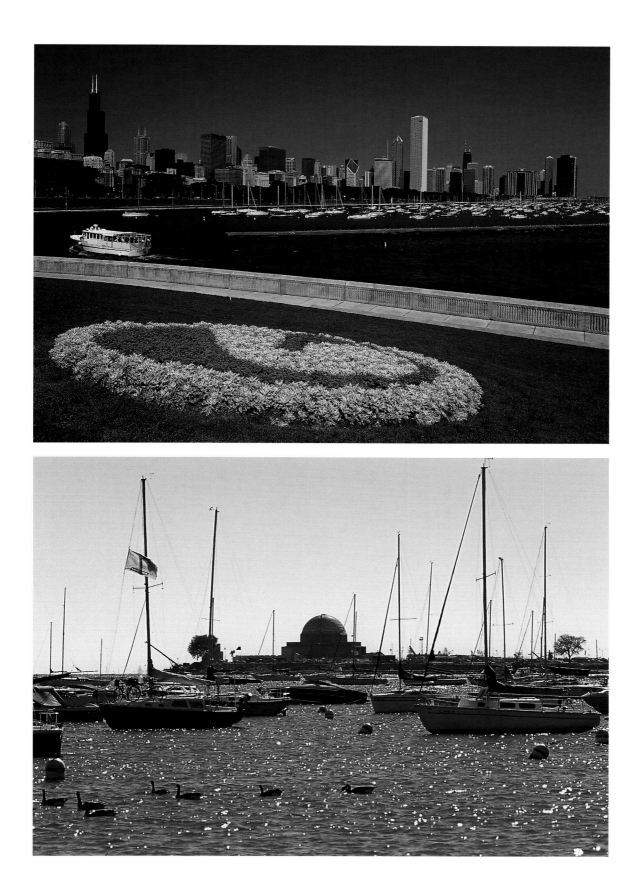

(left) Chicago Yacht Harbor and skyline viewed from Grant Park.

(top) The skyline viewed from across the harbor.

(bottom and overleaf) Adler Planetarium.

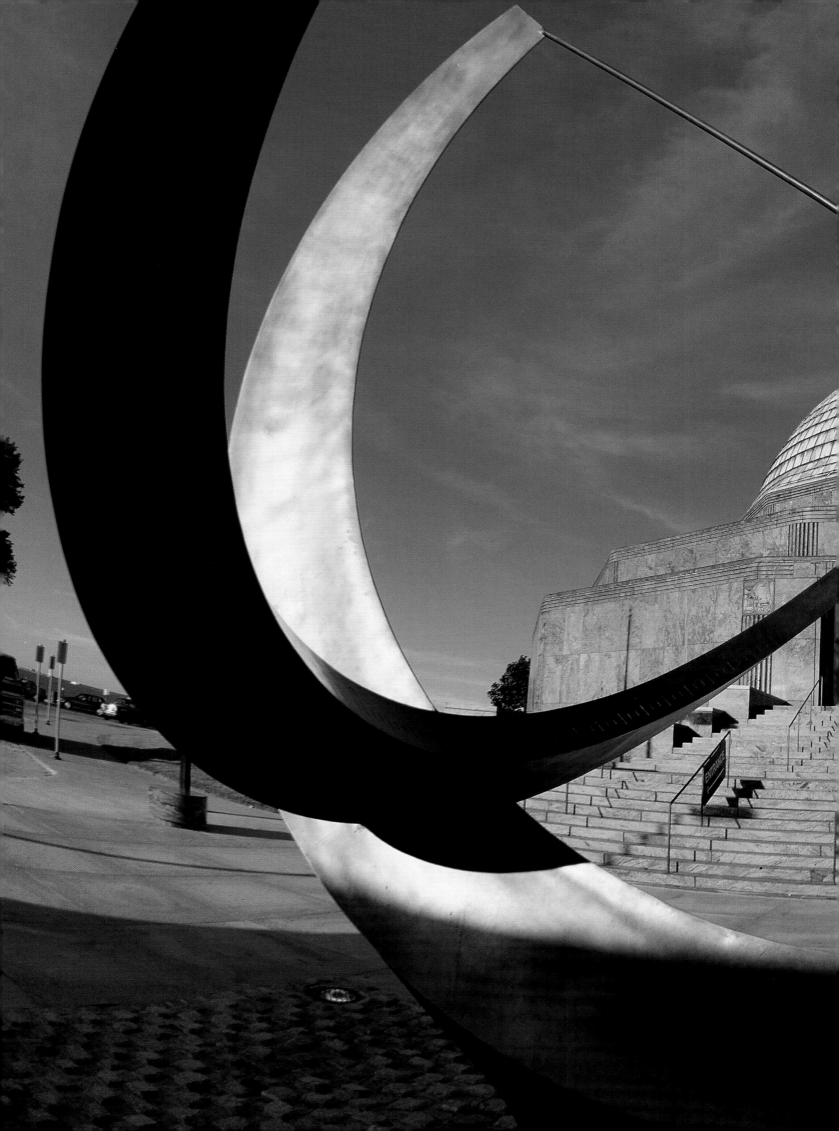

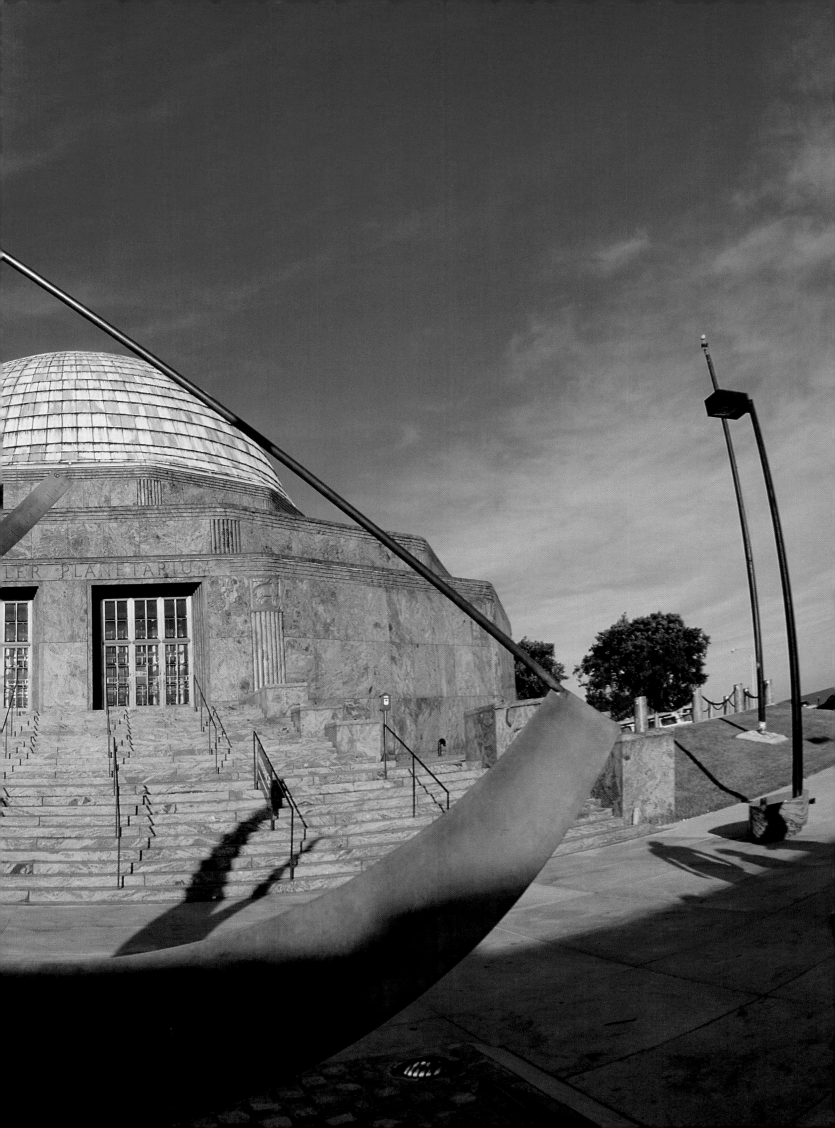

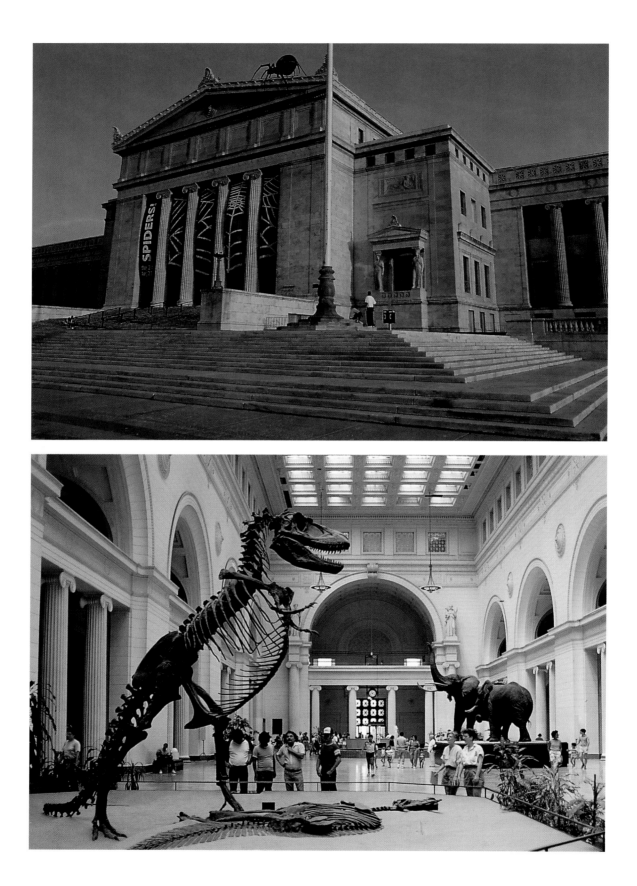

(top) The Field Museum is the largest Georgia marble building in the world, housing some of the finest anthropological, botanical, geological, and zoological collections.

(bottom) Inside the Field Museum—Stanley Field Hall.

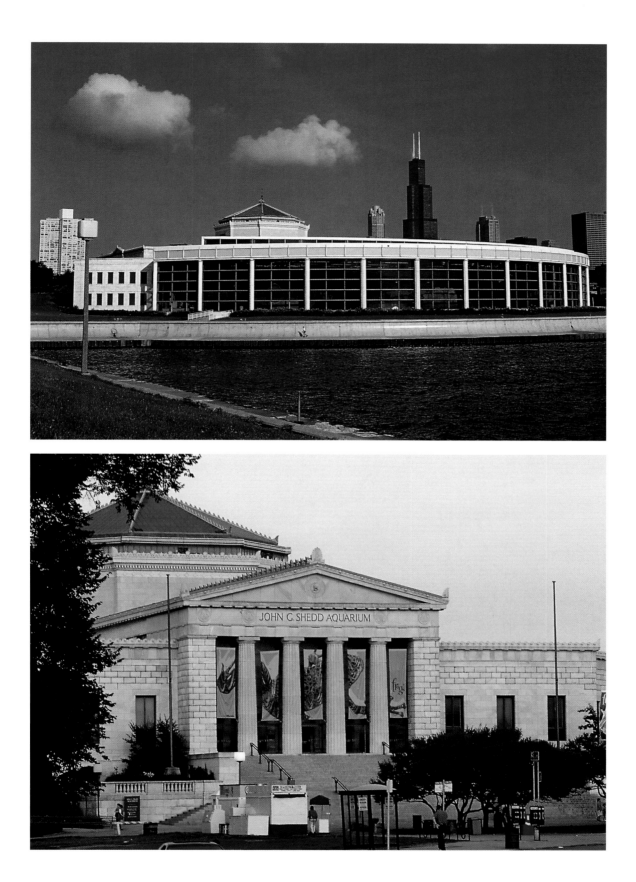

(top and bottom) Shedd Aquarium.

(overleaf) Soldier Field, home of the Chicago Bears.

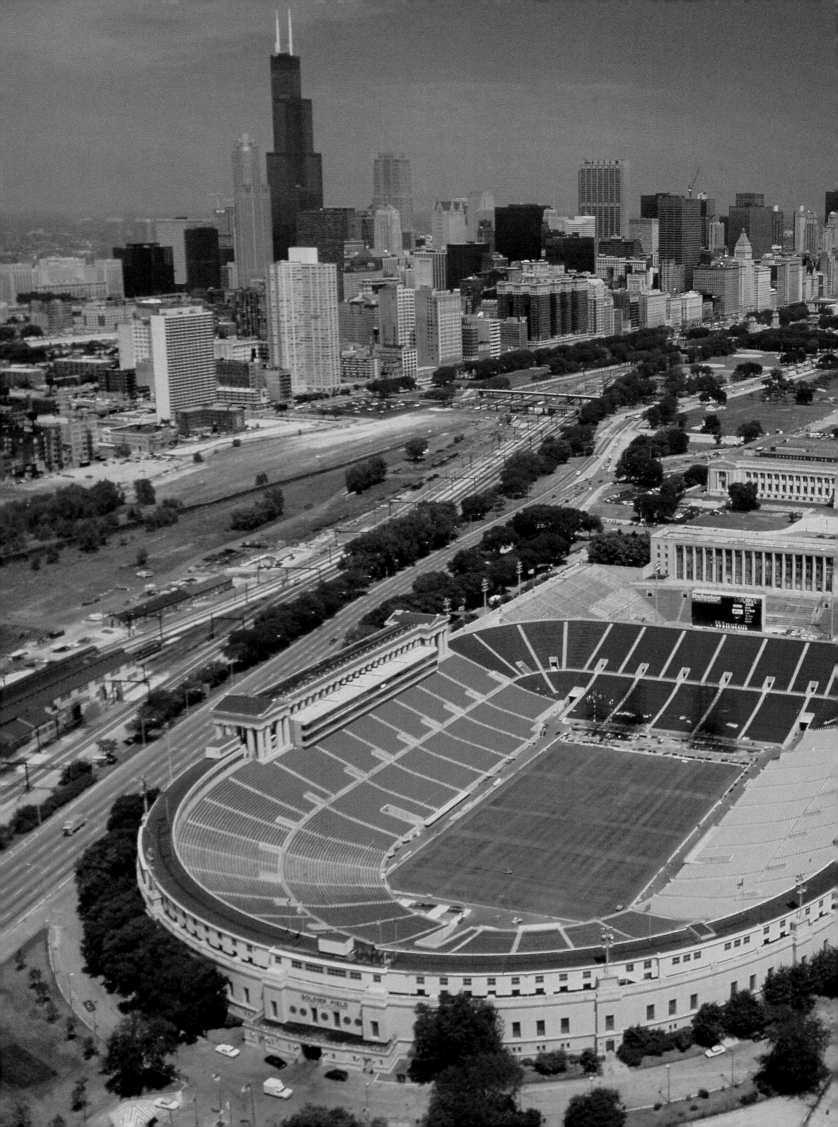

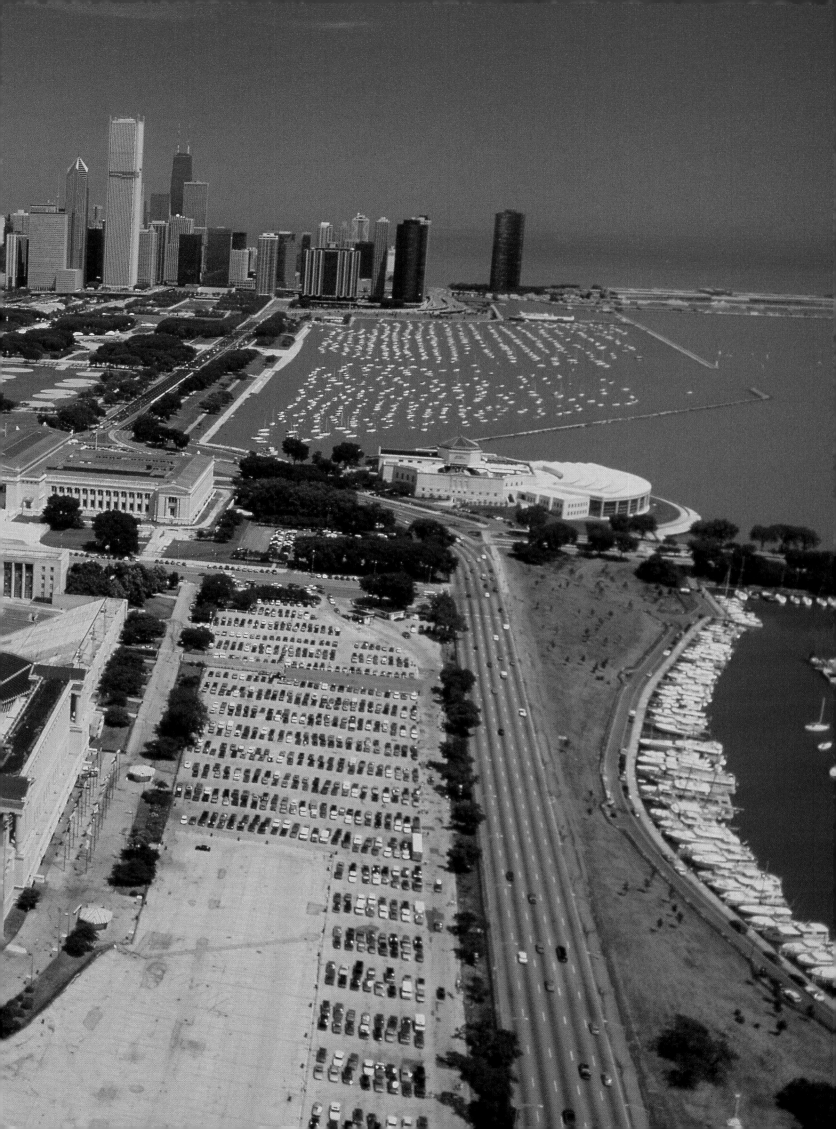

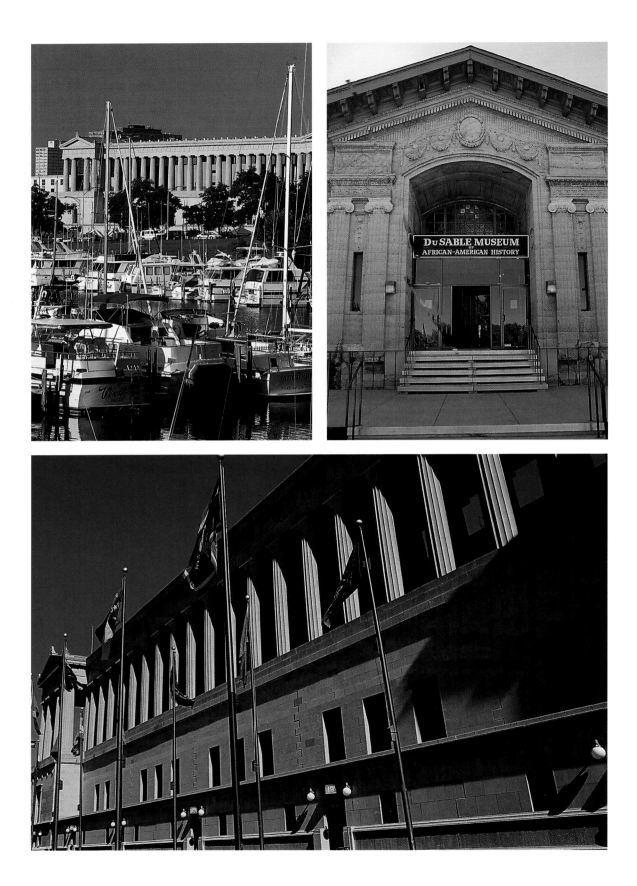

(top left) Burnham Harbor and Soldier Field. **(top right)** The DuSable Museum of African-American History in Hyde Park.

(bottom) Soldier Field. **(right)** The Museum of Science and Industry and Jackson Park lagoon.

(overleaf) The entablature of the Museum of Science and Industry.

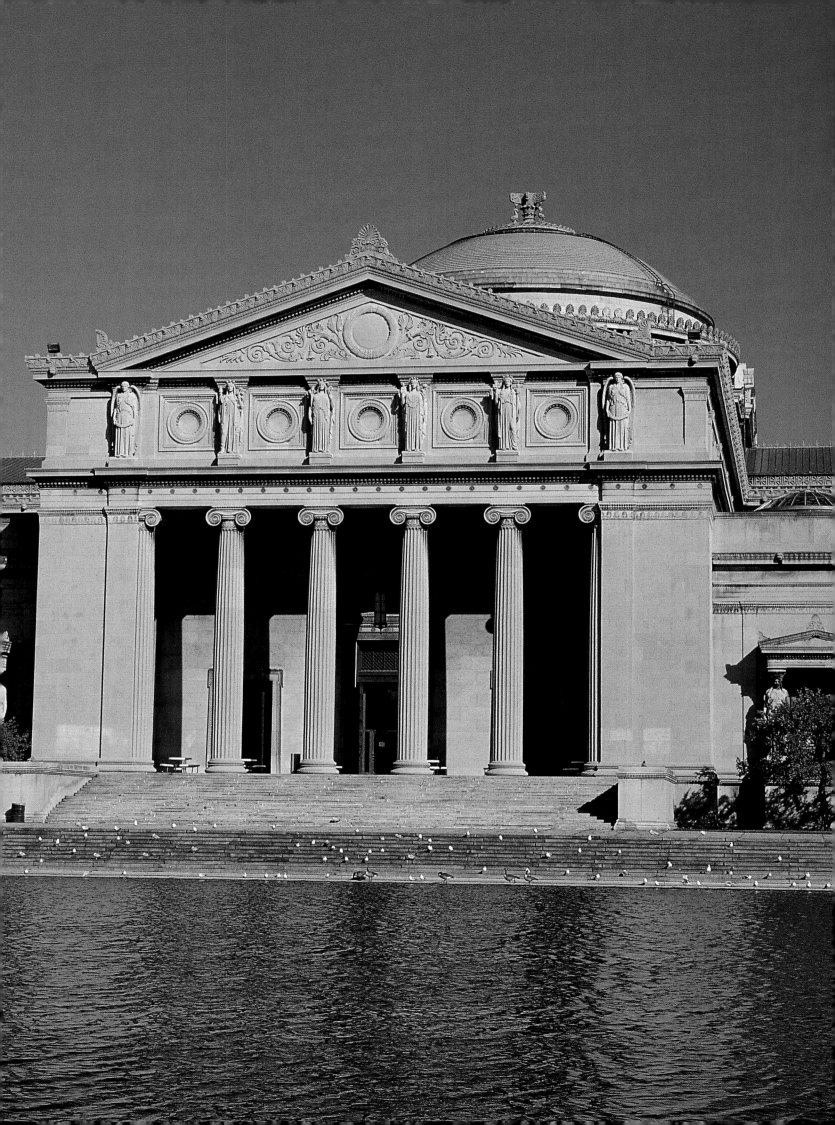

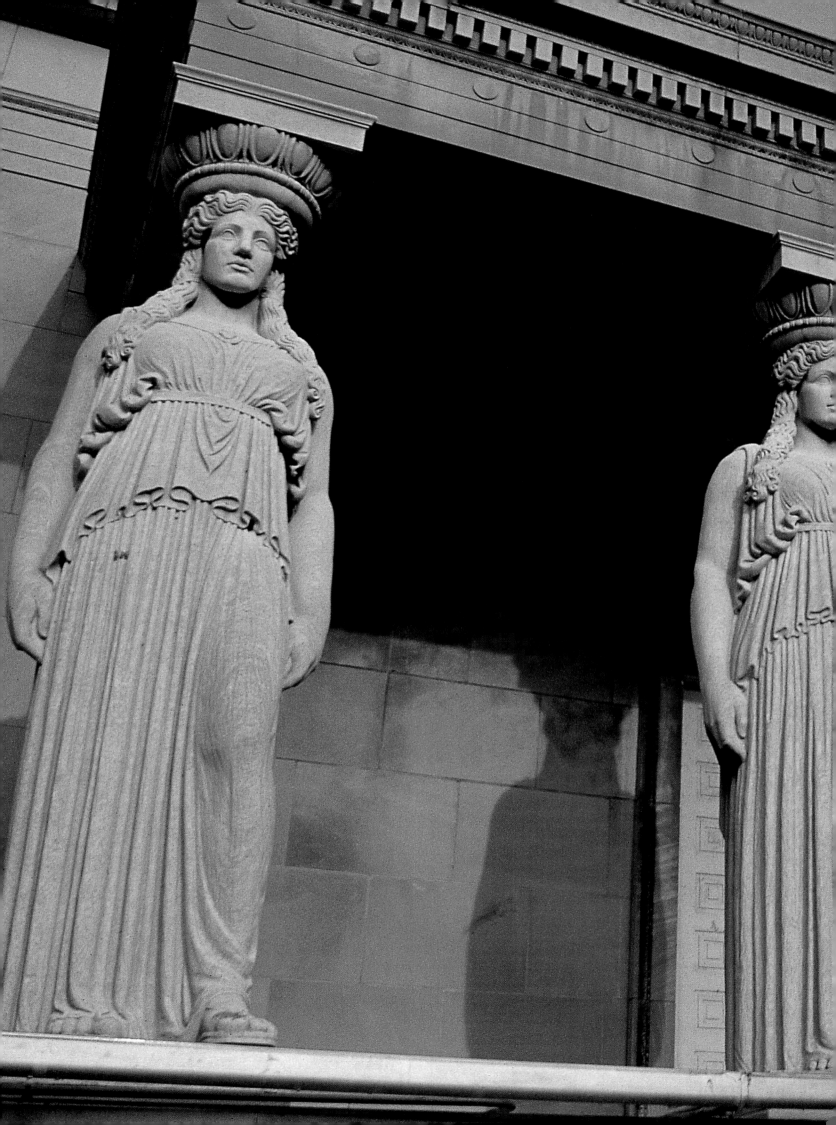

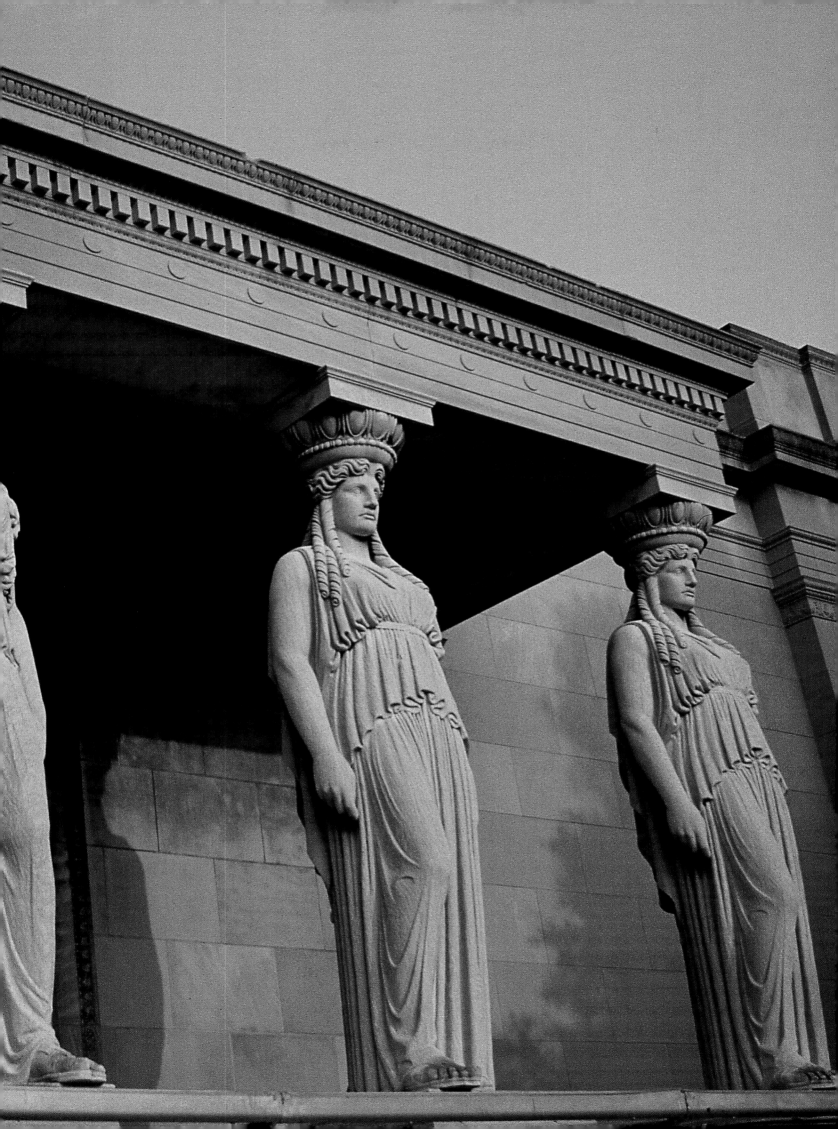

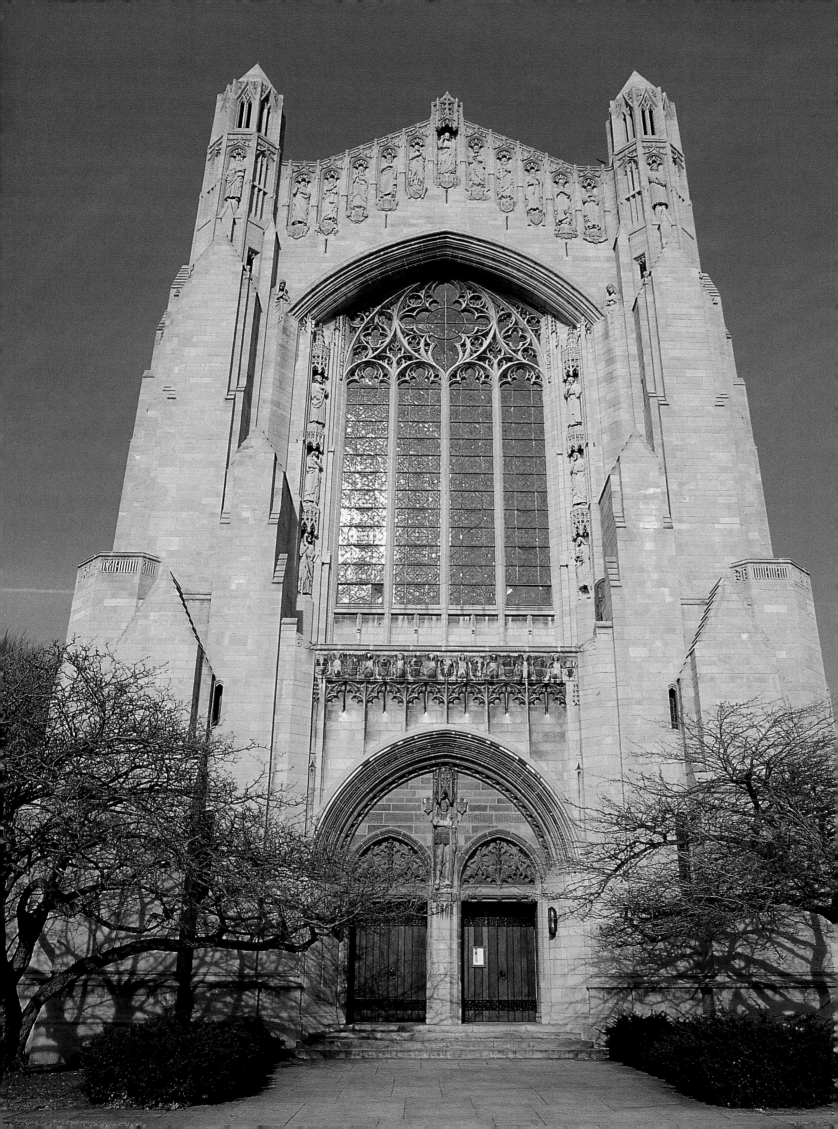

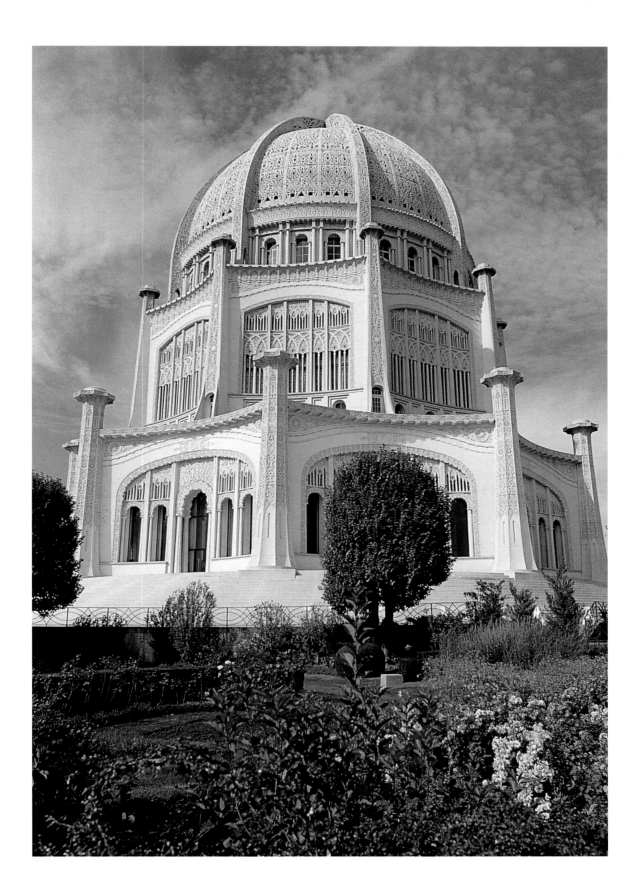

(left) The Rockefeller Memorial Chapel on the University of Chicago campus.

(above) The Bahai House of Worship in Wilmette.

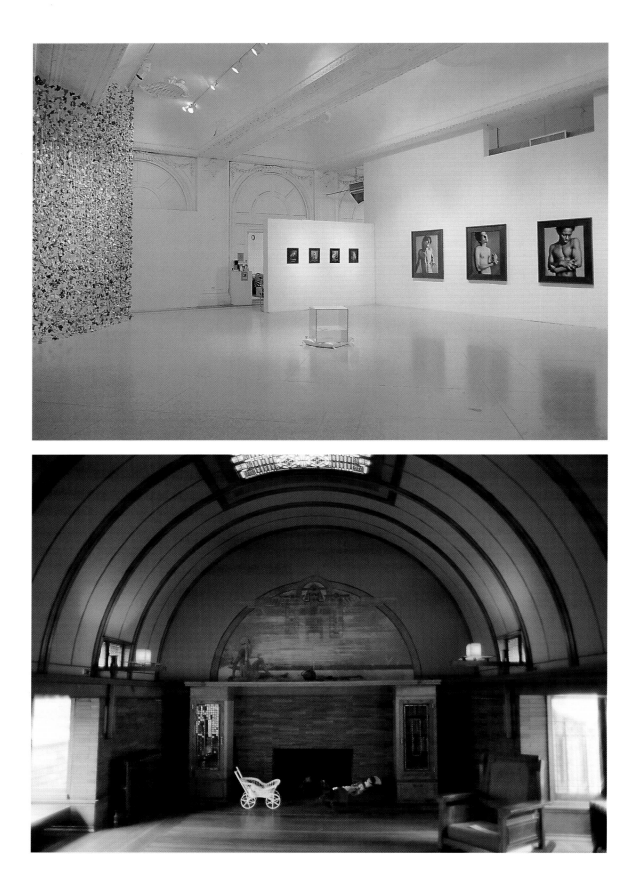

(top) Hyde Park Art Center.

(bottom) Frank Lloyd Wright house.

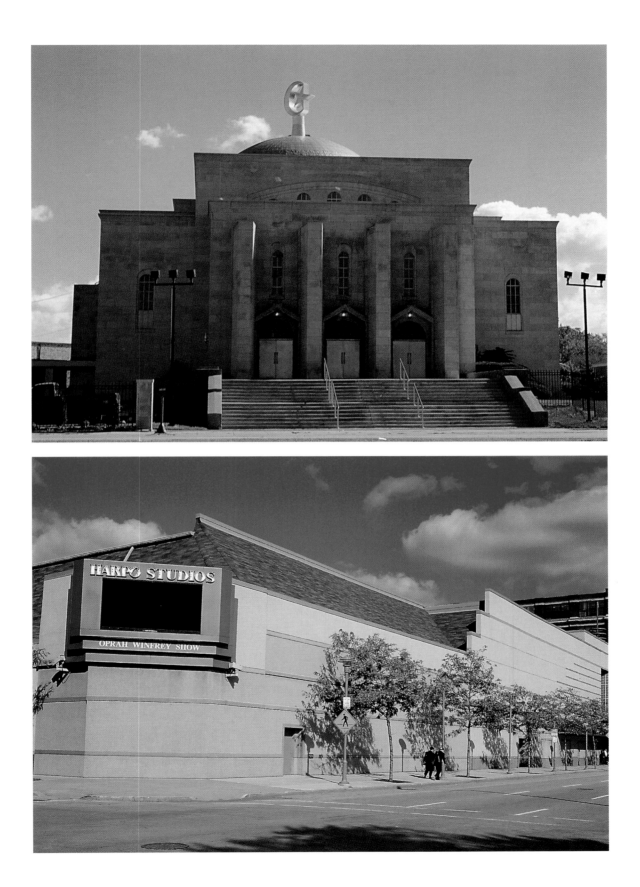

(top) Mosque Maryam on Stoney Island Avenue.

(bottom) Harpo Studio, home of the Oprah Winfrey show.

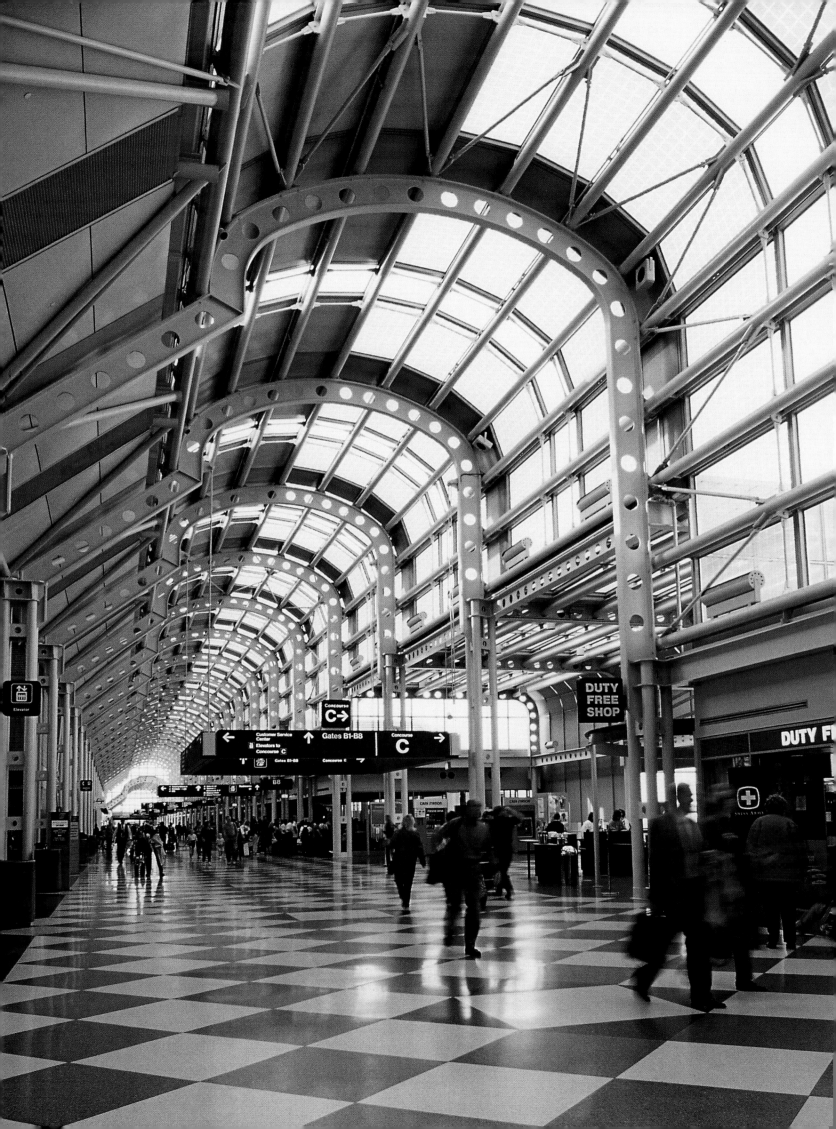

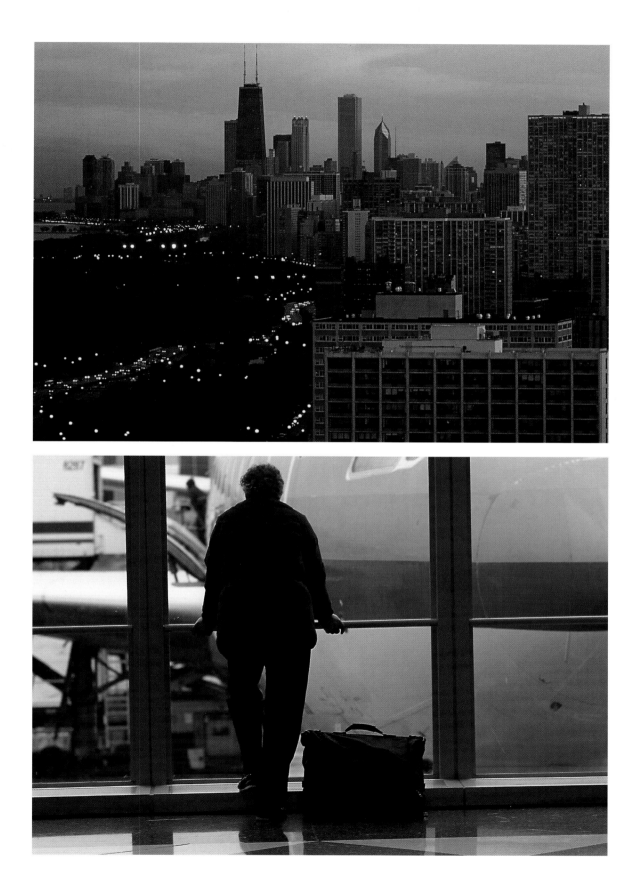

(left) The United Airlines terminal at Chicago's O'Hare International Airport.

(top) The skyline on North Lakeshore Drive.

(bottom and overleaf) Scenes from O'Hare Airport.

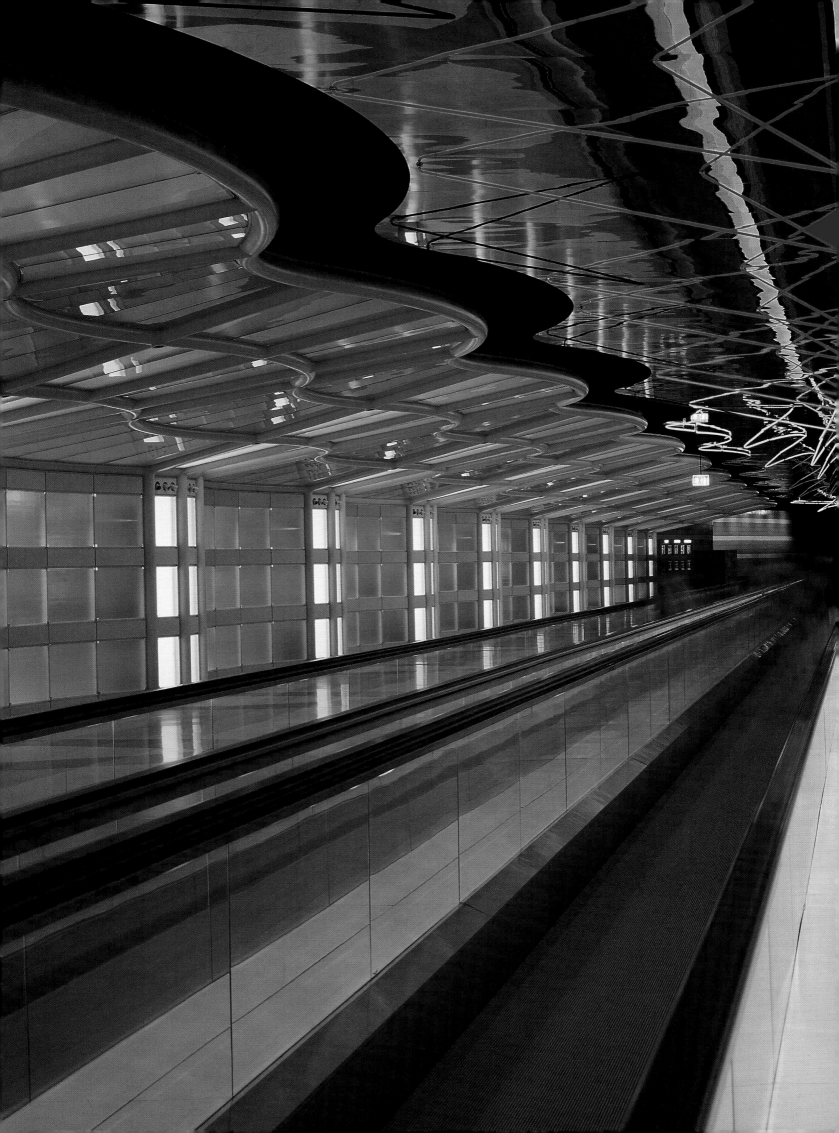

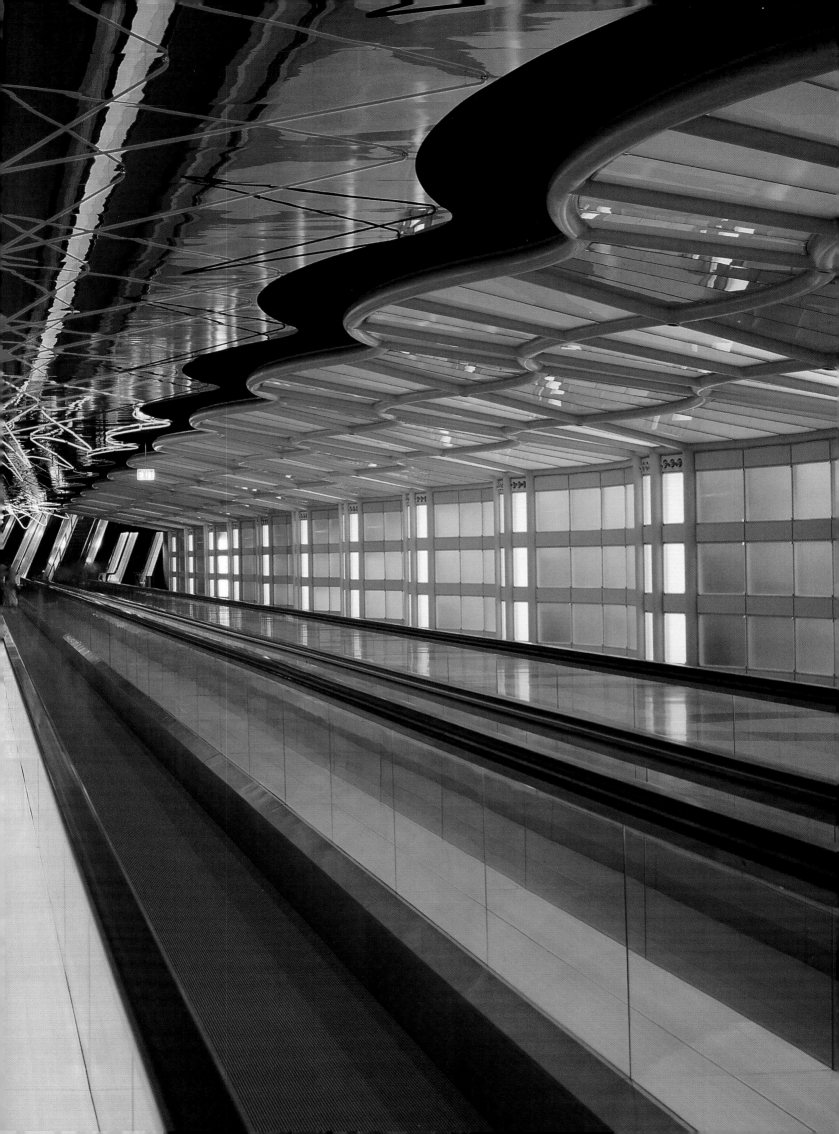

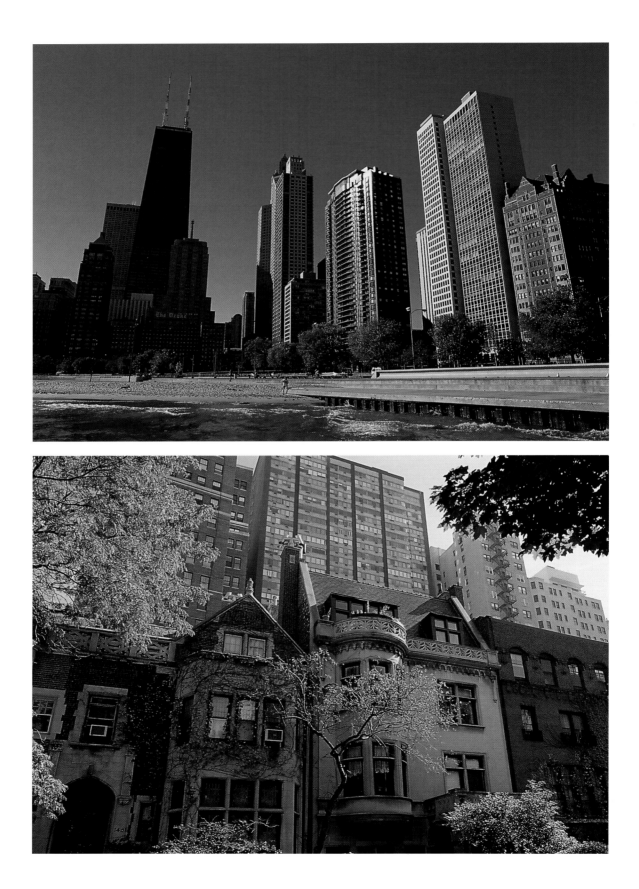

(top) Luxury high-rises and office buildings surround Lakeshore Drive and Oak Street Beach.

(bottom) Townhouses in Romanesque, Revival, and Queen Anne styles line the streets of the "Gold Coast."

(right) Oak Street Beach.

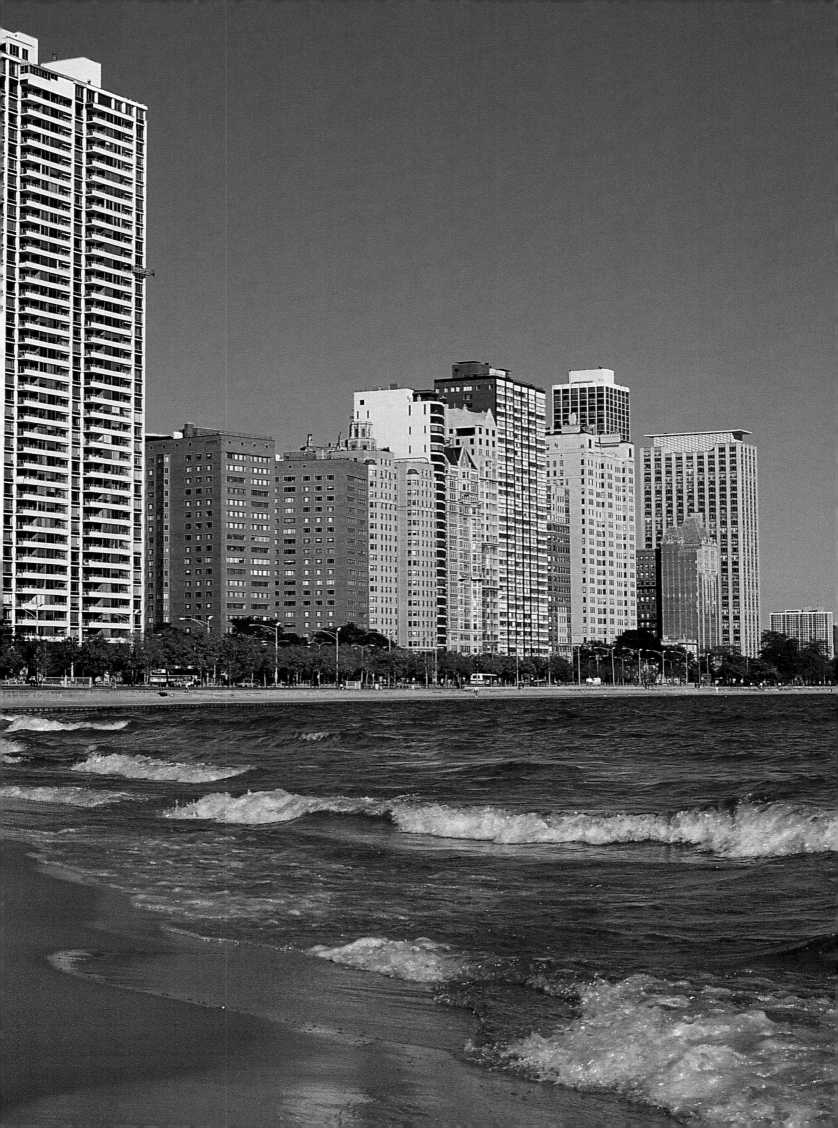

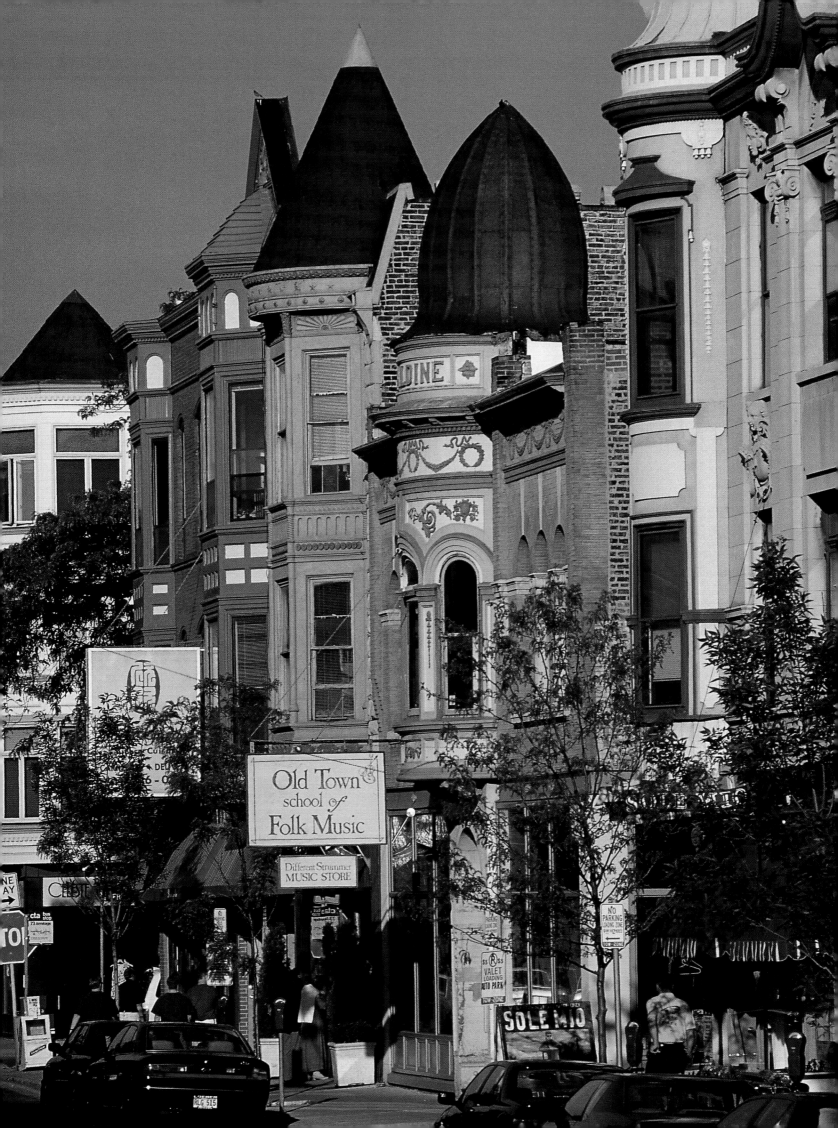

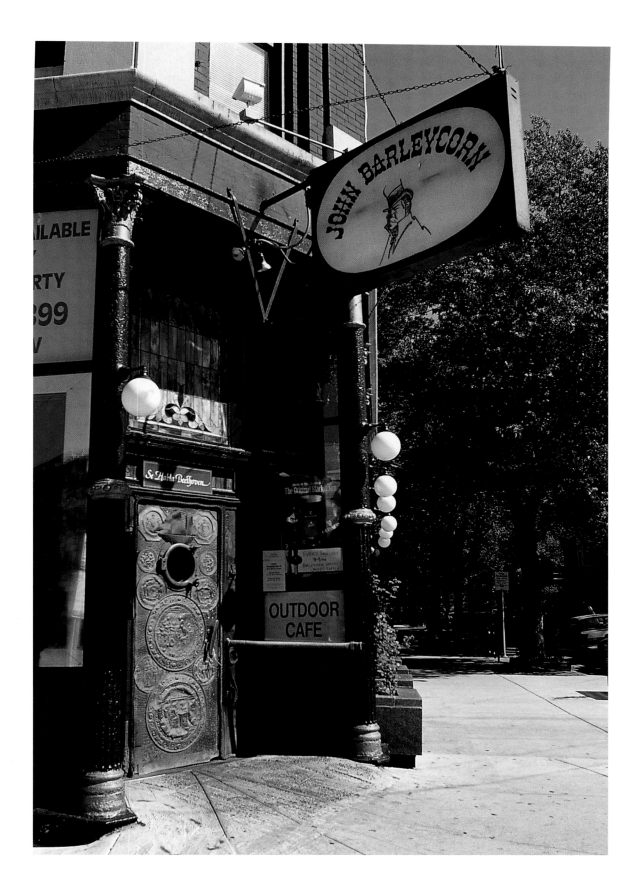

(left) Old Town. (above) The John Barleycorn Memorial Pub, built in 1890, in the Lincoln Park neighborhood.

(overleaf) View from Lincoln Park, looking south toward the city.

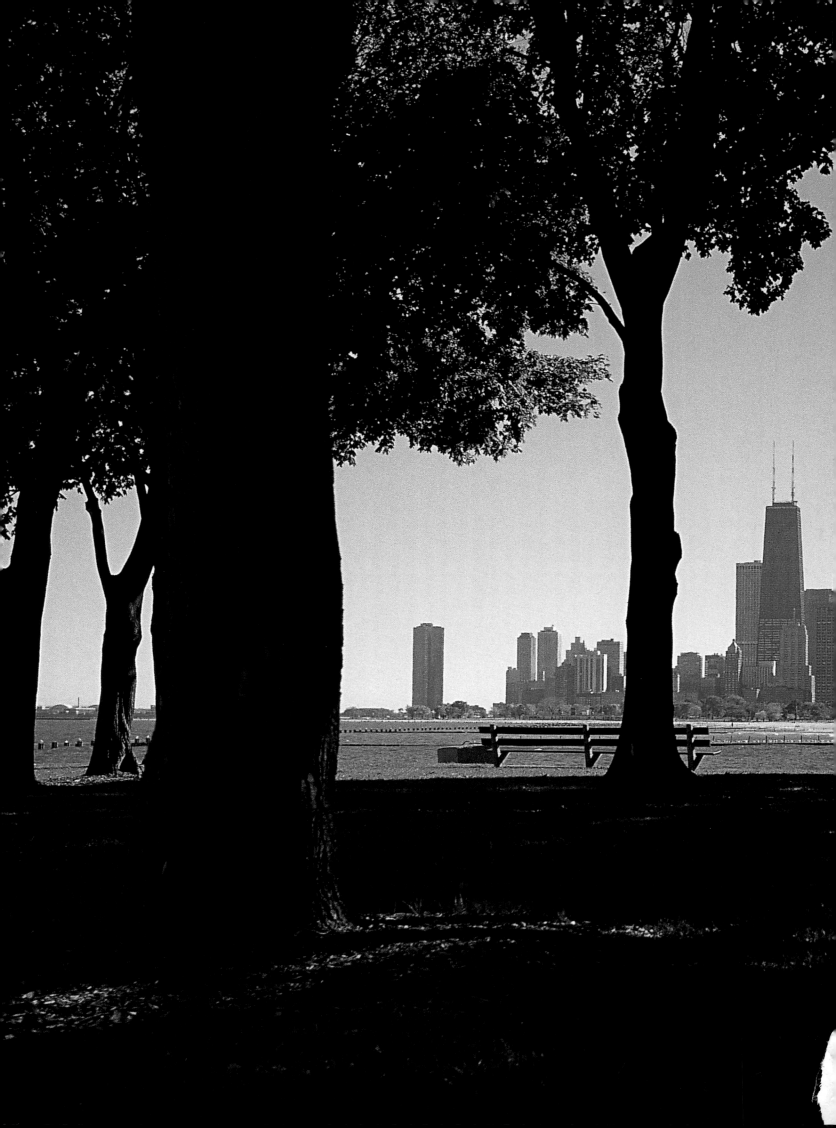

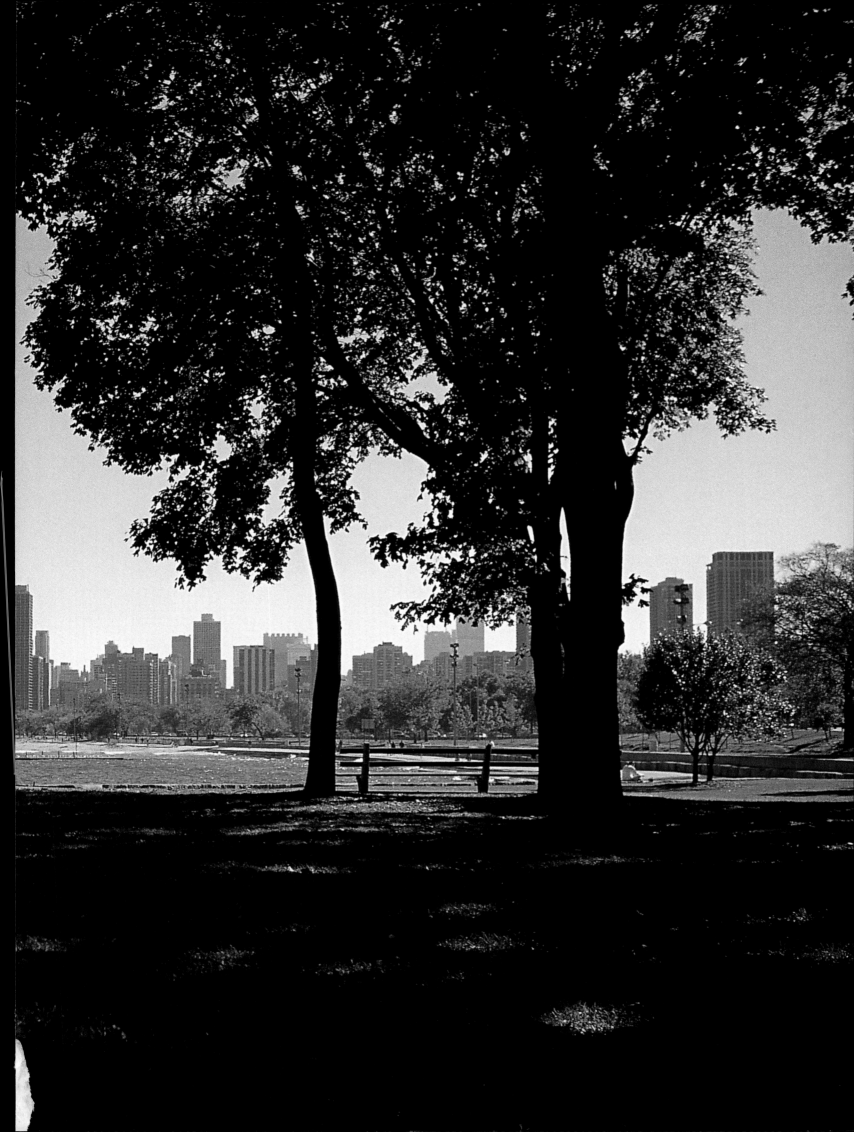

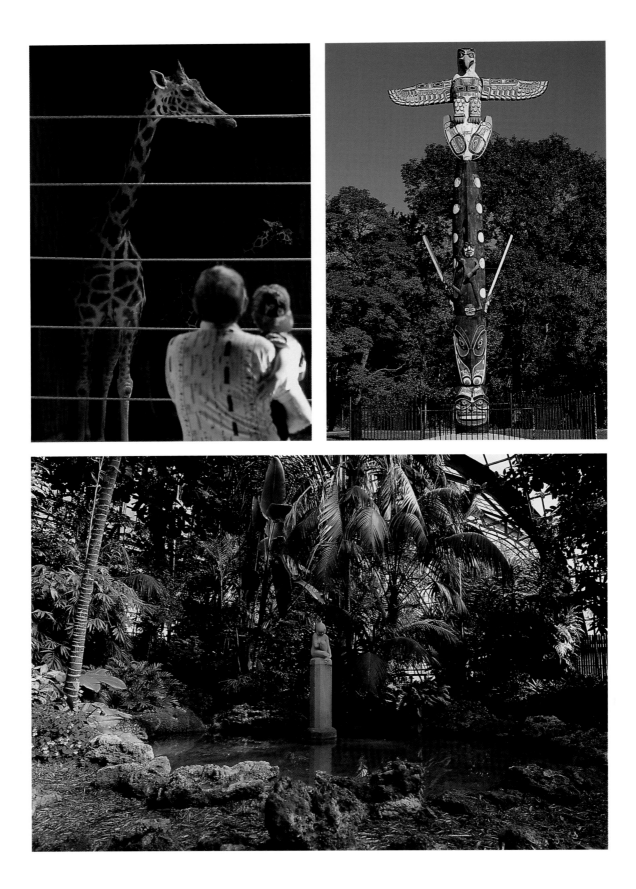

(top left) The Lincoln Park Zoo. **(top right)** "Kwa-Ma-Rolas," a replica in Lincoln Park of a totem pole carved by Kwakiutl Indians at the turn of the century. **(bottom)** Inside the Lincoln Park Conservatory. **(right)** Lincoln Park Conservatory. **(overleaf)** "Storks at Play," a fountain outside the conservatory.

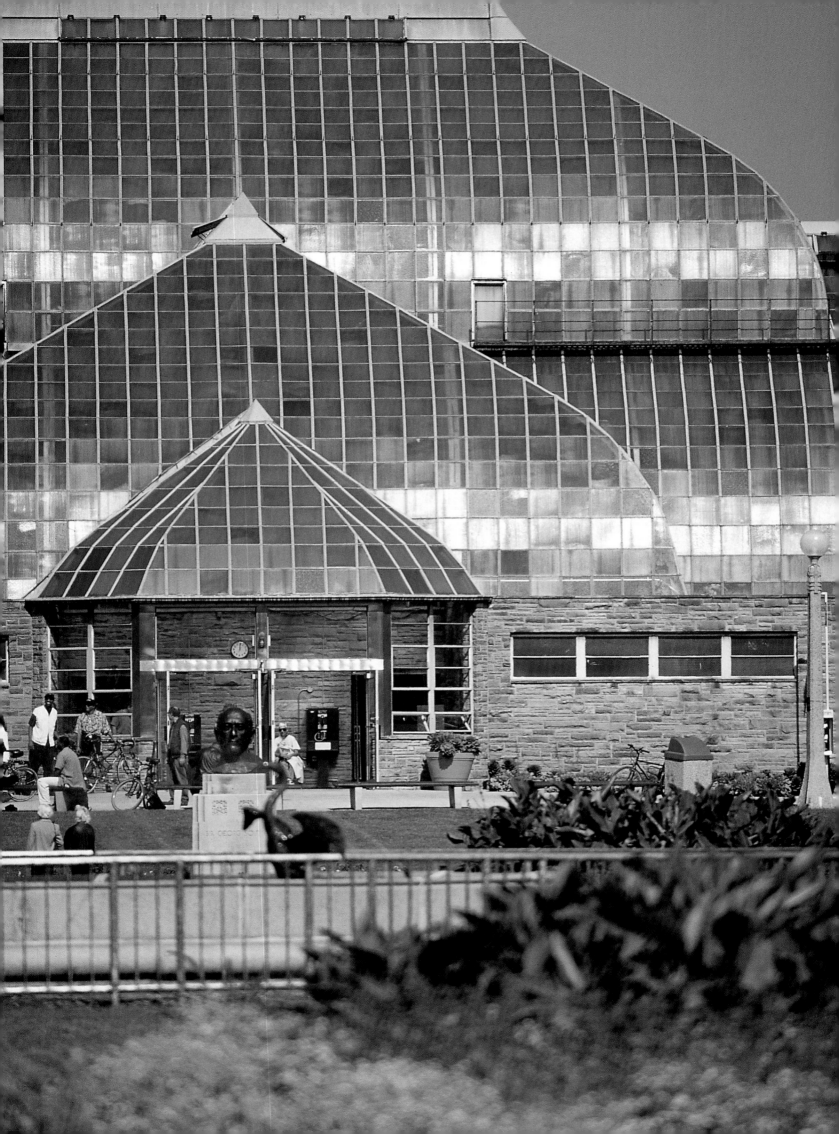

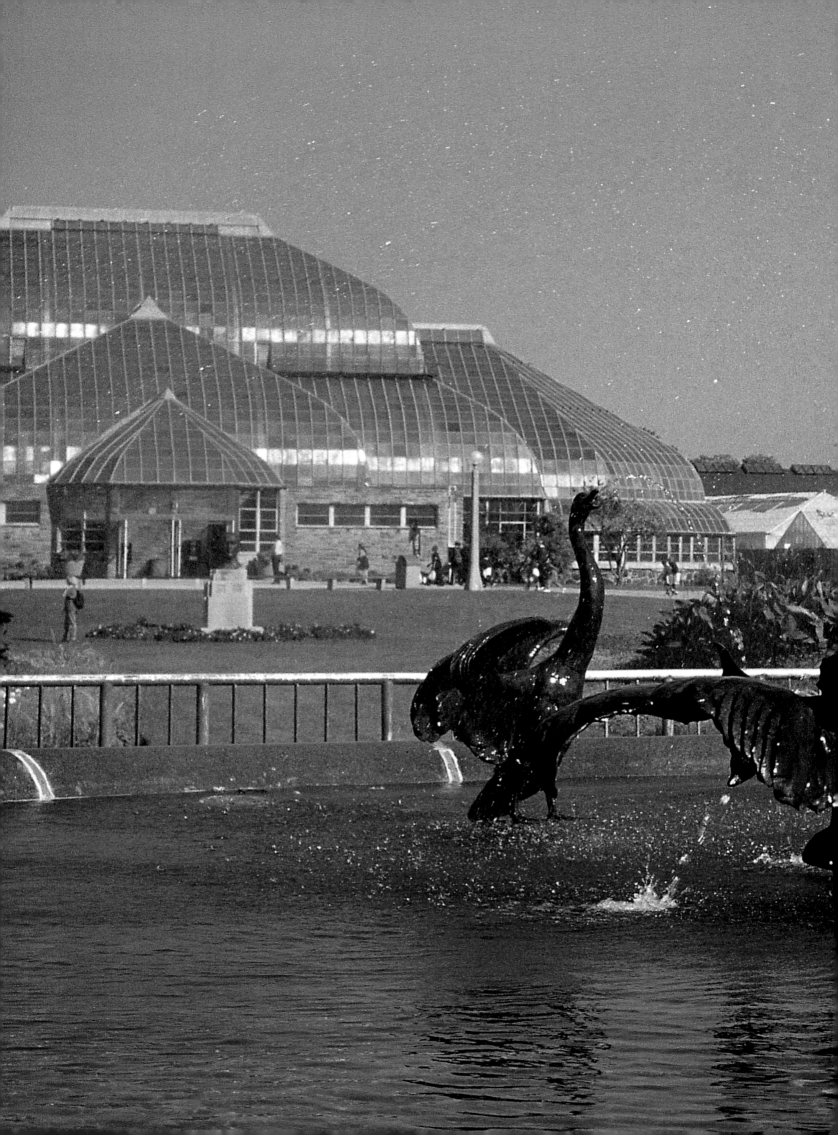

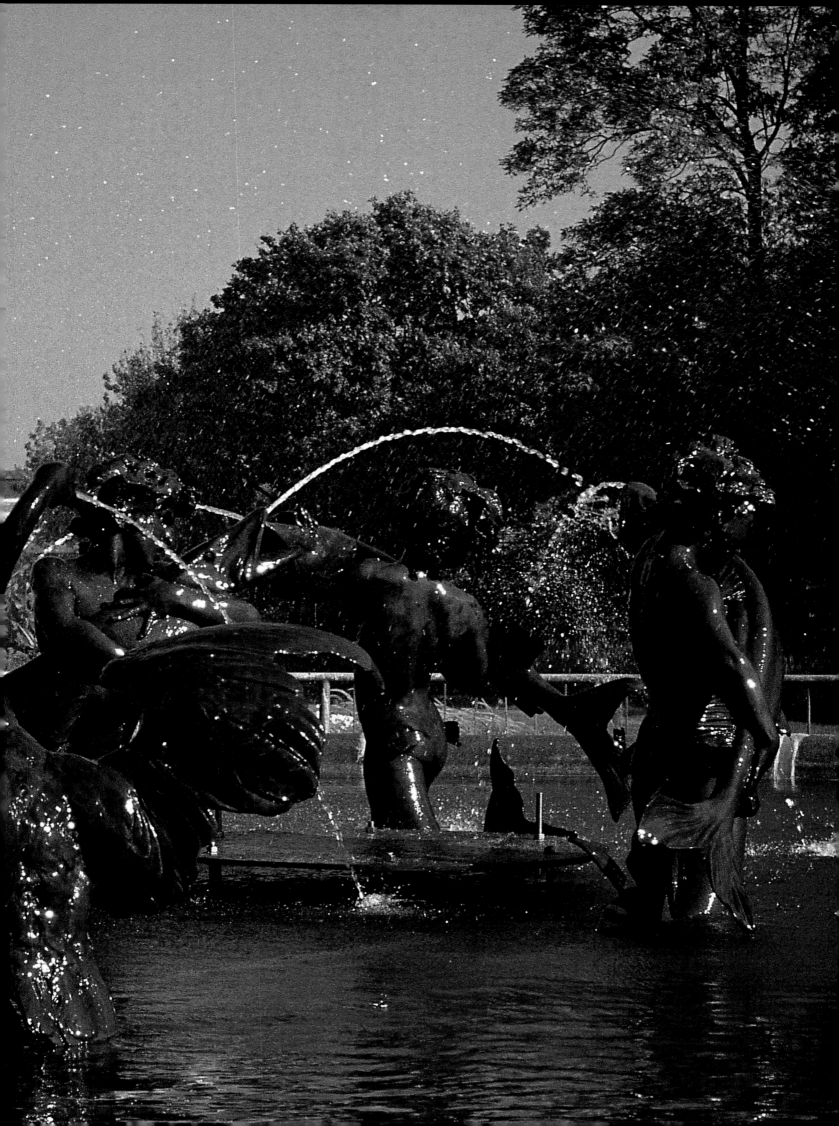

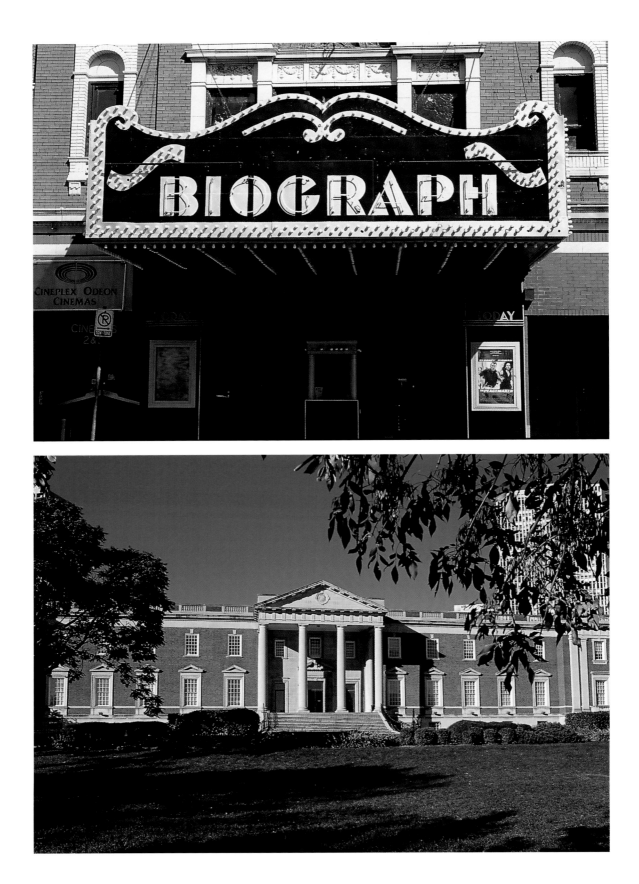

(top) The Biograph Theater, where notorious gangster John Dillinger was fatally shot after a tip-off to federal authorities from a "Lady in Red."

(bottom) The Chicago Historical Society.

(right) The Jane Addams Hull House museum.

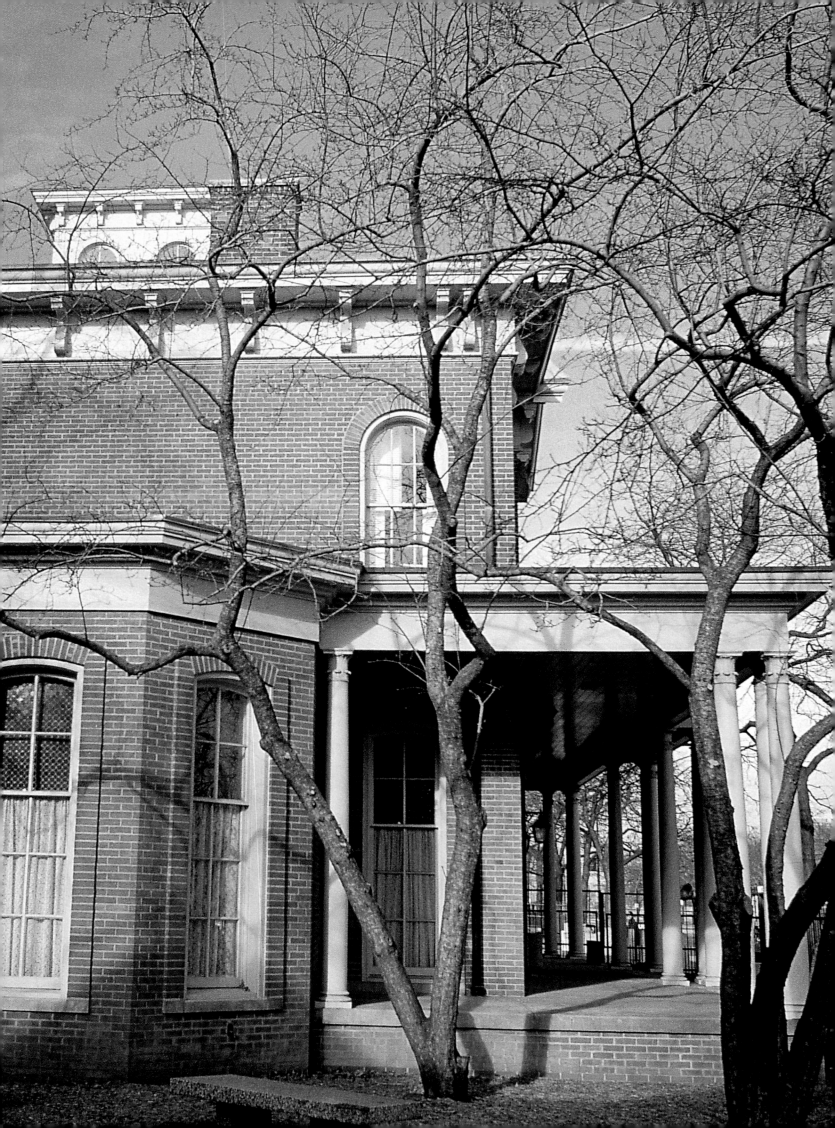

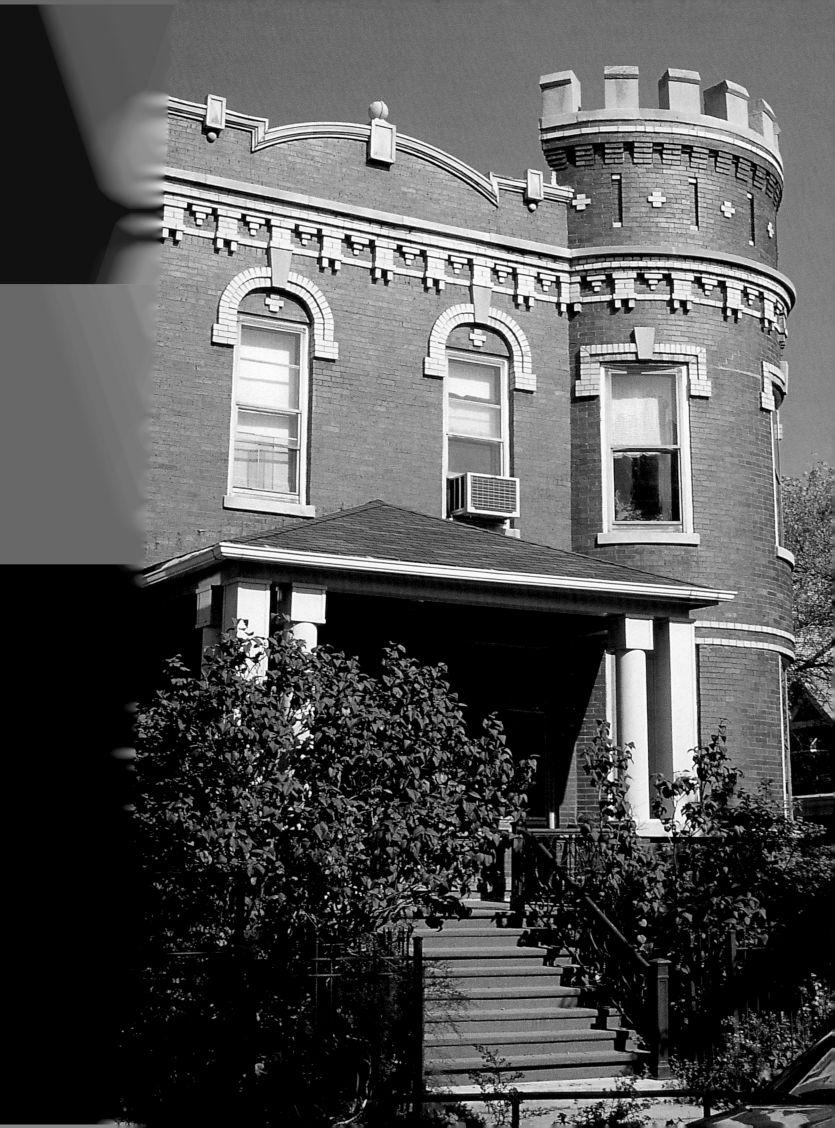

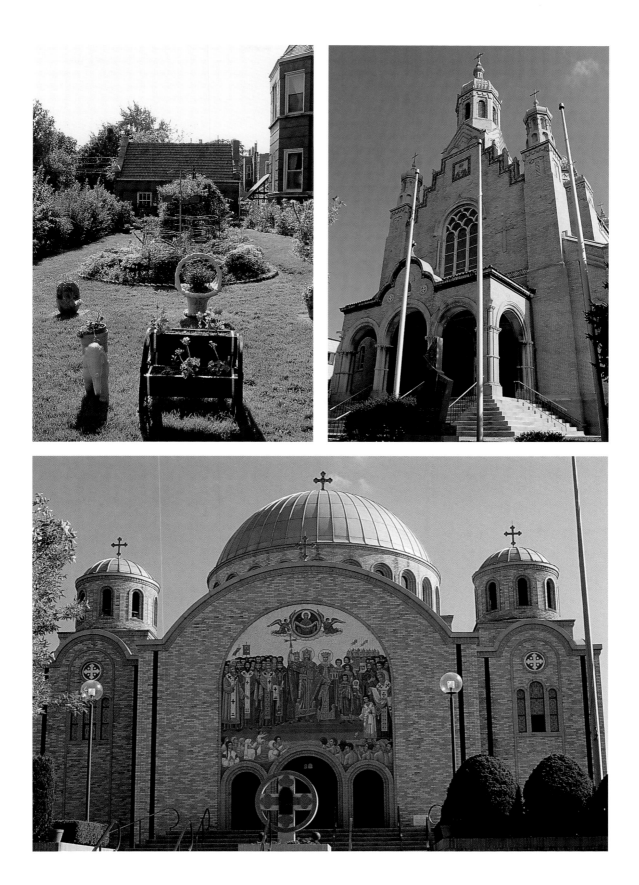

(far left and top left) The Ukrainian Village neighborhood.

(top right) St. Nicholas Cathedral in Ukrainian village.

(bottom) Sts. Volodymyr and Olha Church.

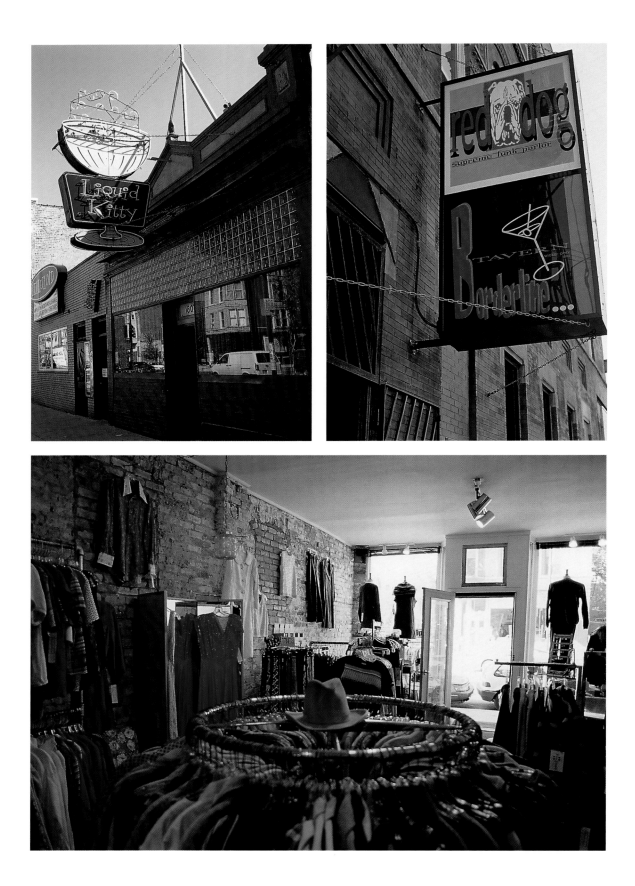

(top left) The Liquid Kitty, a trendy watering hole in Wicker Park.

(top right) The Red Dog dance club and Borderline Bar.

(bottom) You can buy, sell, or trade your vintage 1960s and 70s threads at Dandelion in Wicker Park.

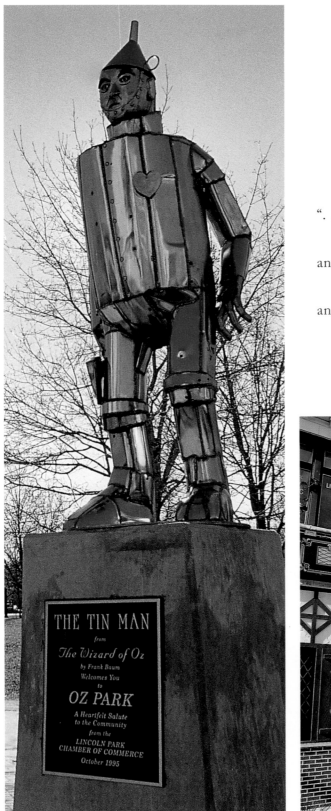

"... to please a child is a sweet

and lovely thing that warms one's heart

and brings its own reward."

—L. Frank Baum

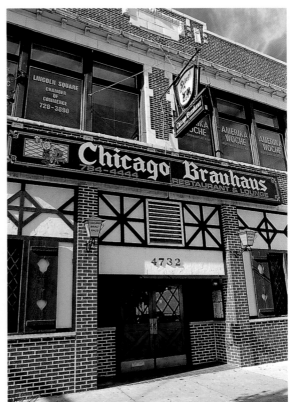

(left) This statue of the Tin Man overlooks Oz Park. L. Frank Baum lived in Chicago when he wrote *The Wonderful Wizard of Oz*.

(right) Chicago Brauhaus in German Town.

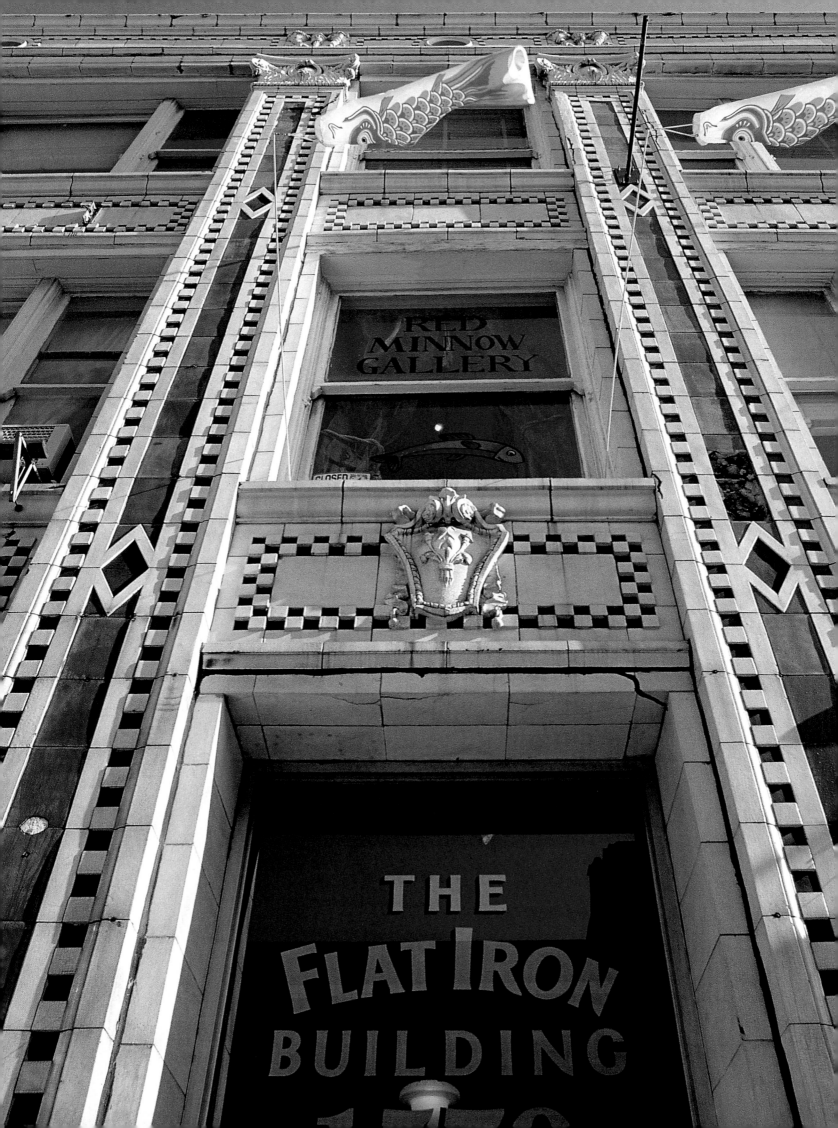

RED
MINNOW
GALLERY

THE
FLAT IRON
BUILDING

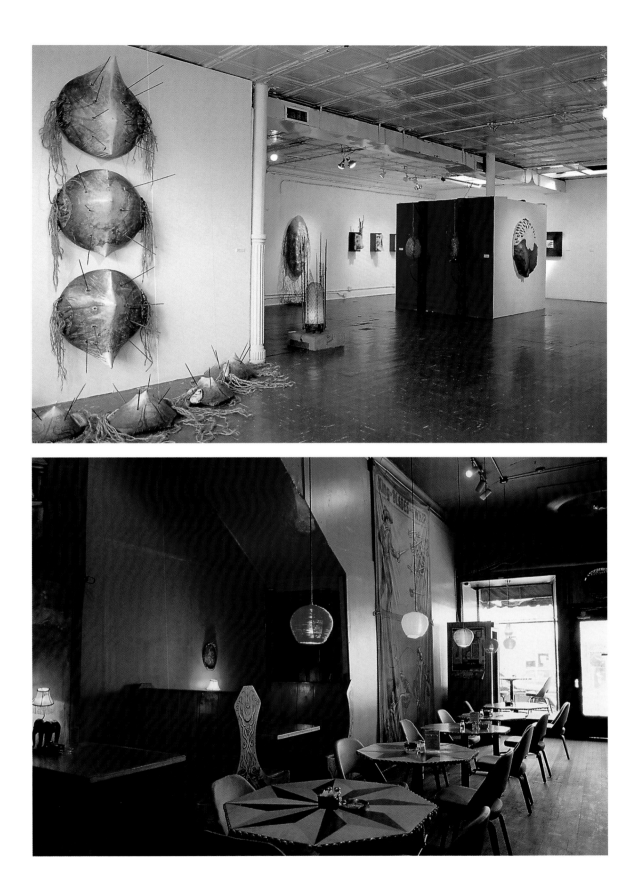

(left) Wicker Park's Flat Iron Building houses art galleries and studios.

(top) The Jorge Felix Exhibition is one of many showcased in the Flat Iron Building.

(bottom) Artists and locals hang out at funky Earwax Cafe.

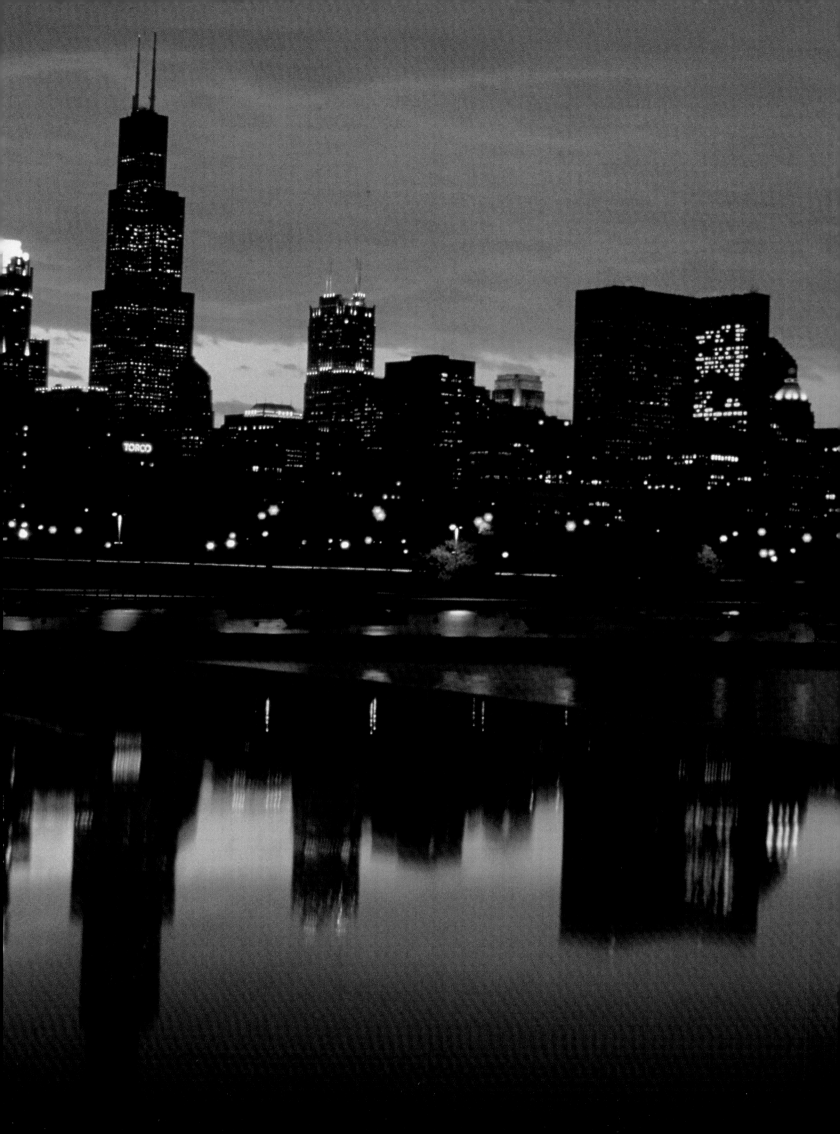

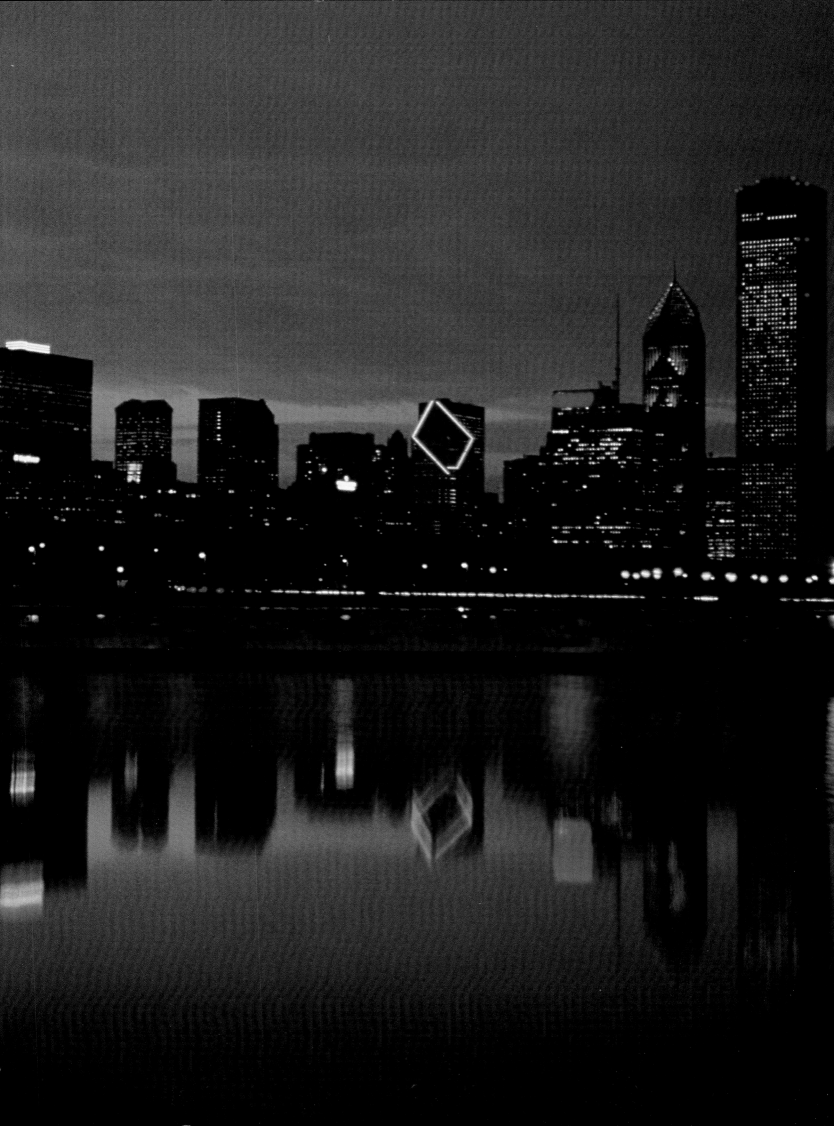

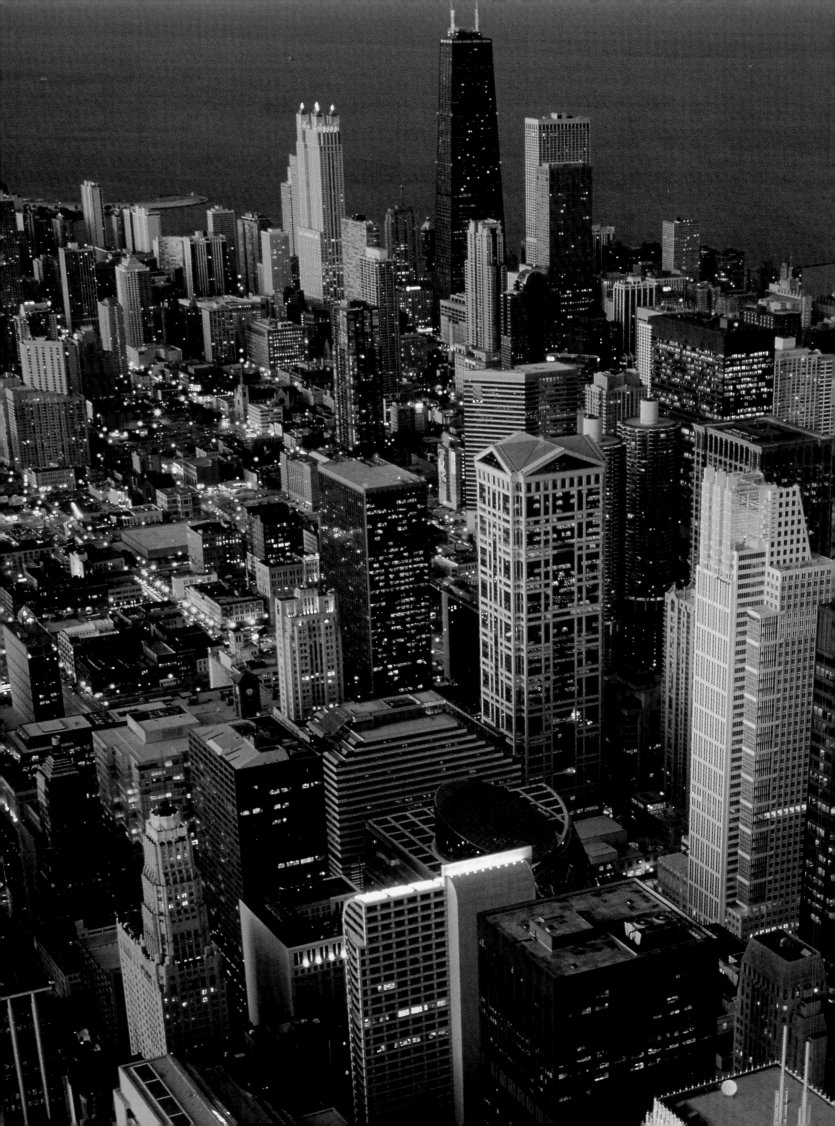